Reading Extra

A resource book of multi-level skills activities

CAMBRIDGE
UNIVERSITY PRESS

Liz Driscoll

CAMBRIDGE UNIVERSITY PRESS
Cambridge, New York, Melbourne, Madrid, Cape Town, Singapore, São Paulo

Cambridge University Press
The Edinburgh Building, Cambridge CB2 2RU, UK

www.cambridge.org
Information on this title: www.cambridge.org/9780521534055

First published 2004
3rd printing 2006

Printed in the United Kingdom at the University Press, Cambridge

A catalogue record for this publication is available from the British Library

ISBN-13 978-0-521-53405-5 Resource Book
ISBN-10 0-521-53405-4 Resource Book

Contents

Map of the book		4
Introduction		7
Thanks and acknowledgements		9
Unit 1	Personal information	10
Unit 2	The family	16
Unit 3	Daily activities	22
Unit 4	Homes	28
Unit 5	Town and country	34
Unit 6	Travel and tourism	40
Unit 7	Food and drink	46
Unit 8	Describing people	52
Unit 9	Describing things	58
Unit 10	Friends and relationships	64
Unit 11	Health and fitness	70
Unit 12	Leisure time	76
Unit 13	Education	82
Unit 14	The world of work	88
Unit 15	Money	94
Unit 16	Past experiences and stories	100
Unit 17	Science and technology	106
Unit 18	Social and environmental issues	112

Map of the book

Theme		Title	Topic	Activity type	Reading focus	Time
1 Personal information						
Elementary	1.1	Write around the world	keypals	read-and-match	reading for specific information, reading for detail	40–50 mins
Intermediate	1.2	The numbers game	names and personal characteristics	read-and-do code-breaking	recognising main ideas, intensive reading	30–40 mins
Upper-intermediate	1.3	Famous last words	what famous people said before they died	matching quotations with people	text cohesion, paraphrasing	40–50 mins
2 The family						
Elementary	2.1	77 years of marriage	longest married couple in Britain	reading comprehension	skimming for text type and topic, scanning for specific words, identifying pronoun references, inferring information from textual clues, text reconstruction	40–50 mins
Intermediate	2.2	What's the best age to get married?	marriage and the best age to do it	note-taking	scanning for names, reading for detail, separating fact and opinion	40–50 mins
Upper-intermediate	2.3	Is that fur comment?	the British and their pets	identifying idioms in a text, working out their meaning	deducing meaning from context	40–50 mins
3 Daily activities						
Elementary	3.1	Where did I see you?	what happened last week	problem solving through groupwork question-and-answer, role play	extracting key information	40–50 mins
Intermediate	3.2	Men who cook	cooking	note-taking	skimming to identify topic, recognising main ideas, reading 'between the lines'	40–50 mins
Upper-intermediate	3.3	Snail mail	snails' addiction to saliva	understanding an authentic newspaper article	deducing meaning, inference, summarising	40–50 mins
4 Homes						
Elementary	4.1	Room to let	accommodation for language students	matching people with accommodation	reading for detail	40–50 mins
Intermediate	4.2	How do you explain that?	urban myths connected with the home	reading about a situation and suggesting an explanation	extracting key information, predicting storyline	40–50 mins
Upper-intermediate	4.3	Hi-tech homes	homes of the future	students make predictions and check them in a text	reading for specific information	40–50 mins
5 Town and country						
Elementary	5.1	What does the sign say?	signs in town and country	understanding signs	understanding main message, identifying function, paraphrasing	40–50 mins
Intermediate	5.2	Where would you prefer to live?	city or country living	note-taking	speed-reading, recognising main ideas	30–40 mins
Upper-intermediate	5.3	Animal city dwellers	wild animals that have been found in cities	completing a text, using clues to work out the content of another text	reading for detail, information gap, recreating a text	40–50 mins
6 Travel and tourism						
Elementary	6.1	Look behind you	urban myth about a terrifying driving experience	ordering a story and suggesting its ending	text organisation	40–50 mins
Intermediate	6.2	Keeping in touch	a trip to New Zealand	ordering e-mails and working out a traveller's itinerary	extracting key information	40–50 mins
Upper-intermediate	6.3	How stupid can you be?	journeys with a difference	separating and ordering stories	speed-reading, text organisation, summarising, recreating a text	40–50 mins

Theme		Title	Topic	Activity type	Reading focus	Time
7 Food and drink						
Elementary	7.1	Putting your eating habits to the test	healthy diets	questionnaire completion	making a personalised response	40–50 mins
Intermediate	7.2	It's not what you eat and drink … it's what you say	food-and-drink quotations	matching beginnings and endings of quotations	sentence structure, paraphrasing	30–40 mins
Upper-intermediate	7.3	How to diet	humorous approach to dieting	prediction and text completion	text structure and coherence, identifying humorous ideas	40–50 mins
8 Describing people						
Elementary	8.1	How do I look?	profile of a circus performer	reading comprehension	skimming for gist, recognising main ideas, text cohesion	40–50 mins
Intermediate	8.2	His or hers?	escape from a prisoner-of-war camp	ordering a story	text organisation	40–50 mins
Upper-intermediate	8.3	What do men really think of cosmetic surgery?	cosmetic surgery	note-taking	reading for detail, identifying topic sentence	40–50 mins
9 Describing things						
Elementary	9.1	Don't go out without your minder	crime prevention product	understanding how a gadget works	using illustrations to deduce meaning, extracting key information	30–40 mins
Intermediate	9.2	Don't forget to pack …	holiday items	matching texts with photos	skimming for general sense, identifying main points	40–50 mins
Upper-intermediate	9.3	Can't live without … bananas	bananas	reading comprehension of an authentic newspaper article	scanning for names, extracting key information, reading for detail	30–40 mins
10 Friends and relationships						
Elementary	10.1	What is a friend?	text based around the word friend(s)	reading and matching	recognising dictionary definitions and separating from examples, speed-reading, scanning for specific words, skimming for text type	40–50 mins
Intermediate	10.2	How to make new friends	ways to meet new people	note-taking	reading for detail, inferring information from textual clues	40–50 mins
Upper-intermediate	10.3	Fiancée loses her ring in Easter egg swap	customs and traditons	reading comprehension	extracting key information	30–40 mins
11 Health and fitness						
Elementary	11.1	Daily wake-up and warm-up	exercise routine	following instructions and carrying out an exercise routine	using illustrations to deduce meaning	30–40 mins
Intermediate	11.2	What shall I do, Doc?	health jokes	matching punch lines with joke questions	sentence structure, paraphrasing	30–40 mins
Upper-intermediate	11.3	'Insane' daredevil skis down Everest	skiing down Everest	understanding an authentic newspaper article	answering your own questions about a text	40–50 mins
12 Leisure time						
Elementary	12.1	A life of leisure	leisure activities	authentic everyday texts	speed-reading, identifying text types from visual clues, reading for specific information	40–50 mins
Intermediate	12.2	The National Museum of Photography, Film and Television	photography, film and television	everyday text (brochure)	reading for specific information	40–50 mins
Upper-intermediate	12.3	Adrenalin capital	extreme sports	getting main points from mini-texts	identifying topic, paraphrasing, choosing titles	40–50 mins

Map of the book

Theme		Title	Topic	Activity type	Reading focus	Time
13 Education						
Elementary	13.1	Cambridge English Readers	using guided readers	pre-reading activities (before reading a reader)	predicting storyline from cover, blurb, chapter headings, list of characters, illustrations, shadow reading	40–50 mins
Intermediate	13.2	Best day, worst day	teacher's best and worst day at school	reading comprehension	reading for main message and to identify writer, deducing meaning of unknown words, paraphrasing, summarising	40–50 mins
Upper-intermediate	13.3	Bacon, ham and eggs	part of a *Just William* story	ordering a dialogue-based story	text organisation, deducing meaning of unknown words	40–50 mins
14 The world of work						
Elementary	14.1	Start your own business	being your own boss	read-and-do	identifying topic area, recognising main ideas, intensive reading	40–50 mins
Intermediate	14.2	It's a risky business	work-related risks	matching related paragraphs	intensive reading, checking predictions	40–50 mins
Upper-intermediate	14.3	Work, sweet work	perks in the work environment	reading comprehension	reading for gist, scanning for specific information, paraphrasing, reading for detail	30–40 mins
15 Money						
Elementary	15.1	You know you're a shopaholic when …	shopping to excess	matching beginnings and endings of humorous sentences	sentence structure, paraphrasing	40–50 mins
Intermediate	15.2	The best and worst … present	giving and receiving presents	note-taking	recognising main ideas, reading 'between the lines'	30–40 mins
Upper-intermediate	15.3	Gold fever	the biggest gold nugget found in Scotland	understanding an authentic newspaper article	extracting key information, creating questions based on a text	30–40 mins
16 Past experiences and stories						
Elementary	16.1	Home and dry	a man's amazing achievement	reading comprehension of an authentic newspaper article	reading for detail, extracting key information, reading 'between the lines'	30–40 mins
Intermediate	16.2	James Cook, navigator	Captain James Cook	matching texts with visuals	scanning for specific words, skimming to identify source, recognising main ideas, note-taking	40–50 mins
Upper-intermediate	16.3	*The Frog Prince* – in the 21st century	a modern version of a traditional tale	ordering a story	text organisation, identifying differences between the modern and traditional tale	40–50 mins
17 Science and technology						
Elementary	17.1	Last man on the moon	space exploration	reading comprehension	scanning for specific words, recognising main ideas	40–50 mins
Intermediate	17.2	Flame and fortune	steelworks re-used as science adventure park	reading comprehension	skimming for gist, reading for specific information	40–50 mins
Upper-intermediate	17.3	Idiotic inventions … and products we could live without	daft inventions	reading a text and choosing a title, using the title to work out the content of another text	extracting key information, asking and answering questions about a text, recreating a text	40–50 mins
18 Social and environmental isssues						
Elementary	18.1	How much do you know about … earthquakes?	earthquakes	problem-solving through pairwork question-and-answer	identifying missing information	40–50 mins
Intermediate	18.2	Mummy, oh Mummy	pollution	ordering lines in a poem	text organisation, understanding the main message	30–40 mins
Upper-intermediate	18.3	Guilty!	lawyer jokes	matching punch lines with joke situations	text cohesion, paraphrasing	40–50 mins

Introduction

Who is *Reading Extra* for?

Reading Extra is a resource book containing photocopiable materials for supplementary classroom work. The activities provide self-contained lessons for the busy teacher. Each activity consists of a page of clear, step-by-step instructions for the teacher and a photocopiable page for the students. The material is aimed at young adult (16+) and adult learners. However, most activities can be easily adapted for the needs of younger students. *Reading Extra* offers teachers an exciting collection of topic-based skills activities from elementary to upper-intermediate level.

How will *Reading Extra* help my students?

In our everyday lives, we read an enormous number and a great variety of things – from theatre tickets to newspaper articles, encyclopaedia entries to recipes, brochures to questionnaires. Yet, students are not always exposed to such a variety of text types in the language classroom. And for this reason, they are not encouraged to read in ways which reflect a genuine purpose in reading.

The materials in *Reading Extra* aim to do two things. Firstly, to give students practice in the reading skills they need in real life, e.g. scanning a TV schedule to find out what time a specific programme is on, skimming a magazine article to identify the writer's opinion, intensive reading of instructions to find out how something works. Secondly, and perhaps more importantly, to give students practice in dealing with unknown words – by using inference from context, general knowledge, morphology – so that they become sufficiently confident to tackle authentic texts, both inside and outside the classroom. While the material has not been written specifically for exam preparation classes, much of it will be suitable for such students.

There are two benefits from working with reading texts in the classroom. The more students read, the better they will read. Furthermore, their knowledge of the language will increase at the same time. For students who are keen to improve their English, reading is the best way forward.

How is *Reading Extra* organised?

Reading Extra is divided into 18 units, each focusing on a different theme. Each unit approaches the theme from an interesting and original angle. The themes cover many of the popular topics found in standard coursebooks. Therefore the activities can be used to supplement existing course material, offering diversity and a refreshing approach to these familiar themes.

Each unit offers three activities at the following levels: elementary, intermediate and upper-intermediate. A map of the book provides a clear overview of the 54 activities, enabling the teacher to quickly locate a suitable activity for their class.

How is each activity organised?

Each activity has one page of step-by-step teacher's notes and a photocopiable sheet on the opposite page for the students.

There is minimal preparation before class. Several activities provide a worksheet for each student, so teachers simply have to photocopy the appropriate number of worksheets.

Sometimes they need to cut up the photocopies – either because students work with a different text each in pairwork or groupwork, or because parts of the text need matching or ordering. For matching and ordering activities, pieces of text should be jumbled and then either held together with a paperclip or stored in an envelope. This may seem time-consuming, but such materials can be used again and again. Students may like to keep a record of the reading they have done – so they may also like a copy of the worksheet in its entirety.

The teacher's notes include a key information panel for quick reference. The headings in this section are:

Level	elementary, intermediate or upper-intermediate
Topic	a brief description of the topic, e.g. healthy diets
Activity type	a brief description of the activity students will be doing and whether they are working in pairs or groups
Reading focus	the particular reading skill that is practised
Time	suggested timing for the Warm up and Main activity (these are only guidelines and timing may vary from class to class)
Key language	vocabulary and structures that students will encounter during the activity
Preparation	what needs to be done before the lesson, e.g. how many photocopies you need to make, what cutting is required, or whether you need to bring anything else to the lesson.

The lesson is divided into three stages:

Warm up	– introduces the topic of the lesson
Main activity	– introduces / revises essential vocabulary items
	– students read the text(s) and carry out related tasks
Follow up	– students make own personalised response to the text(s)
	– students research further reading material about the topic

What is the best way to use *Reading Extra* in the classroom?

The teacher has two roles in the reading classroom. Particularly at the beginning of the lesson, the teacher is at the centre of the action – initiating discussion, handing out materials, giving instructions, checking feedback. But, while the reading is actually going on, the teacher's role is that of monitor, supporter and advisor. It is the students themselves who must do the reading!

But this does not mean that the reading classroom should be a silent place. In the real world, we often discuss things we have just read. Similarly, we ask for clarification if there is something we have not understood. To reflect the real world, and to encourage the on-going process of learning, allow and encourage students to work together in pairs while they are reading the same text.

A well-equipped reading classroom should provide each student with easy access to an English/English dictionary such as the *Cambridge Advanced Learner's Dictionary*. At the same time, students should be encouraged to turn to the dictionary to look up an unknown word only as a last resort or to check their prediction – they have the context of the word to help with its meaning, they have their classmates to offer support and advice, they have the teacher to point them in the right direction.

Reading need not be confined to the classroom, however, and suggestions for further reading are provided where appropriate as a Follow up activity. For those students who are studying in an English-speaking country, there is reading material in abundance. And for students who are studying in their own country, library books, readers and newspapers, etc. are often available. Furthermore, the Internet provides an easily accessible source of reading material.

This book is part of a family of skills books in the Cambridge Copy Collection series. The other books available are *Listening Extra*, *Speaking Extra* and *Writing Extra*, and they each follow a similar format.

Thanks and acknowledgements

The author would like to thank Nóirín Burke of Cambridge University Press who commissioned the project, and Frances Amrani, also of Cambridge University Press, who provided help, guidance and support as she edited the material.

The author and publishers are grateful to the following individuals who reviewed and piloted the material with their students during its development:

Vladimir Jungova, Prague, Czech Republic; Magda Laurence, Cairo, Egypt; Ingrid Lecoq-Gellerson, Riehen, Switzerland; Gordon Robinson, Singapore; Kevin Rutherford, Warsaw, Poland; Sarah Schechter, Cambridge, UK; Roger Scott, Bournemouth, UK; Roy Sprenger, Troyes, France; Tamara Stanivska, Kiev, Ukraine; Wayne Trotman, Izmir, Turkey; Rob Waring, Okayama, Japan; Andrew Wright, Gödöllo, Hungary.

The authors and publishers are grateful to the following copyright holders for permission to reproduce copyright material. While every endeavour has been made, it has not been possible to identify the sources of all material used and in such cases the publishers would welcome information from copyright sources. Apologies are expressed for any omissions.

p.15: extract from *Famous Last Words* by Jonathan Green, published by Kyle Cathie; p.17: extract from 'A lasting love' by Bill Mouland, published *Daily Mail* (8 February 2002) © Atlantic Syndication; p.21: 'Is that fur comment?' © Justine Hawkins, published *The Guardian* (2 February 2002), and p.27: 'Lurking inside the postbox: snail mail' by John Vidal, published *The Guardian* (10 November 2001), and p.33: 'Geekhouse' © Marc Ambasna-Jones, published *The Guardian* (2 February 2002), and p.39: 'Big snapper takes bite of Big Apple', reprinted by permission of Michael Ellison, published *The Guardian* (17 June 2000), and 'Koalas try suburban jungle', reprinted by permission of Patrick Barkham, published *The Guardian* (26 May 2001), and p.61: 'Kepi hat' published *The Guardian* (15 May 2002), 'TV specs' published *The Guardian* (25 May 2002), 'Tempur pillow' published *The Guardian* (20 April 2002) © Tim Wapshott, and p.63: 'Can't live without … bananas', © Sally Kinnes published *The Guardian* (6 July 2002), and p.69: 'Fiancée loses her ring' by Philip Willan, published *The Observer* (15 April 2001); and p.75: 'Insane daredevil' by Paul Harris, published *The Observer* (8 October 2000), and p.81: for the article 'Adrenalin capital' adapted from 'Ultimate Highs', published *The Guardian* (8 December 2001) with permission of Judy van der Walt, p.85: 'Best day, worst day' © Eileen Sheridan published *The Guardian* (6 July 2002), and p.99: 'Gold fever', adapted from 'Hopefuls head for the hills' by Kirsty Scott published *The Guardian* (6 July 2001), and p.101: 'Home and dry' by Jeevan Vasagar, published *The Guardian* (24 April 2002), and p.109: 'Flame and fortune' by Stephen McClarence published *The Observer* (9 April 2001) Guardian Newspapers Limited; p.25: extract from 'Men who cook' featured in *Sainsbury's Magazine*, (April 2002), New Crane Publishing Ltd.; p.31 and p.45: extracts taken from *The Best Book of Urban Myths – Ever* by Yorick Brown and Mike Flynn (1998) published Carlton; p.41: 'Look behind you' and p.65: 'What my friends would change about me' extracts from *Shout* (11-24 January 2002) © D.C. Thomson & Co Ltd; p.47: 'Putting your eating habits to the test' and p.71: 'Daily wake-up and warm-up', extracts from *Get Fit Feel Fantastic* by Anne Hooper and Michael Perring, published by Carrol & Brown Publishers Limited; p.49: 'It's not what you eat and drink' from *Food Lovers: Quotations for lovers of their tummy'*, published Country Studios, reprinted by permission of History & Heraldry Ltd.; p.49: quote by George Bernard Shaw, with permission of the Society of Authors on behalf of the Bernard Shaw Estate; p.51: 'How to diet' with permission of Guy Browning; p.53: 'How do I look', by Caroline Wingfield first published in *The Independent* (25 May 2002) © Independent Newspapers (UK) Ltd.; p.57: 'What do men really think of cosmetic surgery', written by Alison Palmer, published in *Woman* magazine (6 May 2003); p.59: 'Don't go out without your minder', with permission of JNE Marketing Ltd. www.jnemarketing.co.uk; p.65: Dictionary entry for 'friend', from the Cambridge International Dictionary of English (2001) edited by Patrick Gillard, and p.65: from *Just Good Friends* by Penny Hancock (1999), and p.83: Cambridge English Readers, published by Cambridge University Press; p.65: with permission of Friends of the earth International. http://www.foei.org/; p.65: Friends Membership Card, with permission of The Oxford Playhouse. http://www.oxfordplayhouse.com/; p.77: Programme, with permission of the Phoenix Picturehouse, Oxford; p.77: Train timetable, with permission of Thames Trains; p.79: extracts from the brochure of The National Museum of Photography, Film and Television. http://www.nmpft.org.uk; p.87: 'Bacon, ham and eggs', adapted extract from *William the Pirate* by Richmal Ashbee, with permission of A.P. Watt Ltd.; p.89: 'Start your own business' with permission of Shell Livewire. www.shell-livewire.org Telephone: 0845 757 3253; p.91: 'It's a risky business', extract from *The book of chance: Your guide to the Risks of Modern Living*, by John Hodgson published by Weidenfeld & Nicolson; p.93: 'Work, sweet work' from *Egg* brochure, with permission © Egg; p.95: 'You know you're a shopaholic when …' by Michelle Leggatt published (2001), Summersdale Publishers Ltd.; p.103: 'James Cook, navigator', brochure and maps with permission of Captain Cook Tourism Association. www.captaincook.org.uk; p.105: 'The Frog Prince – in the 21st century', from *Politically Correct Bedtime Stories* (1994) by James Finn Garner © Souvenir Press Ltd, and John Wiley & Sons, Inc.; p.107: 'Last man on the moon' adapted from 'Return of the moon walkers' written by Jonathan Leake, *The Sunday Times* © NI Syndication London (12 May 2002); p.113: 'How much do you know about … earthquakes?', reproduced from *Facts and Lists* by permission of Usborne Publishing, 83-85 Saffron Hill, London EC1N 8RT. Copyright © 1987 Usborne Publishing Ltd.

The authors and publishers are grateful to the following photographic sources: *Daily Mail*, © Caters News: p.17; *Sainsbury's Magazine* © New Crane Publishing Ltd.: p.25 (photo Nicky Johnston); Associated Press Worldwide Photos: p.39 tr; © Stephen Saks/Lonely planet Images: p.39; *The Independent* (25 May 2022) © Independent Newspapers: p.53 (photo Andrew Fox); Design-Go: p.61 (Belt bank); Travelling Light. www.TravellingLight.com: p.61 (Kepi hat); Tempur UK. www.physiosupplies.com: p.61; (Transit pillow); GVR Products Limited. www.reddylite.com: p.61 (Recumbent spectacles); PAN Advertising Agency: p.75; logo © NFPTM: p.79; Wallace and Gromit © Aardman/W&G Ltd 1989; (Dolphins) © Ecoscene, photographer Visual and Written: p.79; Bond logo, courtesy of NMSI touring exhibition curated by National Museum of Photography, Film and Television: p.79; The Museum of Lead Mining. www.leadminingmuseum.co.uk: p.99; Flora, London Marathon. http://www.london-marathon.co.uk: p.101; (Eugene Cernan) © Science Museum/Science and Society Picture Library: p.107; Magna Trust. http://magna.livewwware.com: p.109.

Illustrations: Asa Anderson (pp.27, 63, 69) Phill Burrows (pp.13, 31, 65); CSL Cartoonstock (p.51); Terry Finnegan (p.11); Tony Forbes (p.113); Hardlines (pp.35, 36, 41, 59, 61, 103); Martin Smith (pp.37, 71, 115); Sam Thompson (pp.29, 67); Jonathan Williams (p.43); Debbie Hinks (p.83).

Text design: HL Studios, Fenlock Court, Long Hanborough, Oxford

Page make-up: HL Studios, Fenlock Court, Long Hanborough, Oxford

Cover illustration: Tim Kahane

Cover design: HL Studios, Fenlock Court, Long Hanborough, Oxford

The publisher has used its best endeavours to ensure that the URLs for external websites referred to in this book are correct and active at the time of going to press. However, the publisher has no responsibility for the websites and can make no guarantee that a site will remain live or that the content is or will remain appropriate.

1.1

Write around the world

LEVEL
Elementary

TOPIC
Keypals

ACTIVITY TYPE
Read-and-match

READING FOCUS
Reading for specific information, reading for detail

TIME
40–50 minutes

KEY LANGUAGE
Present tense of *be*

PREPARATION
One photocopy for each student

Warm up

1 Write the word *keypal* on the board. Elicit or explain that a *keypal* is someone you exchange e-mails with as a hobby but whom you usually haven't met. Encourage students to talk about any keypals or penfriends that they write to.

Main activity

1 Explain to students that they are going to read descriptions of keypals.

2 Give each student a photocopy. Read the introduction and look at the chart with the class. Encourage students to work out the meaning of any unknown headings from the information already in the chart.

3 Ask *Who is 24?* Students read the descriptions quickly in order to answer the question. Explain that one piece of information is given about five of the people; the completely empty section of the chart is for the sixth.

4 Ask students to read the descriptions and complete the chart. Encourage students to work together in pairs so that they can help each other.

5 Check the answers with the class. Ask a question using the information already given in the chart to identify each person, e.g. *Who is Polish?* Then ask *How old is she? Where is she from? What is her job? What are her hobbies?*

Answer key						
name	Paulo Dias	Maria Szopen	Claudette Romand	Stefan Zilliken	Mikhael Pavlov	Belén Lopez
age	**24**	21	25	23	20	22
nationality	Brazilian	**Polish**	French	German	Russian	Spanish
home city	Rio de Janeiro	Warsaw	**Lyons**	Munich	Moscow	Madrid
job	teacher	computer programmer	ski instructor	**travel agent**	student	nurse
hobbies	water sports, music	cinema, running	travel photography	football, walking	**computer games, Internet**	sport, eating out

6 Tell students to underline the phrase or sentence which refers to the picture.

Answer key
Belén: I like eating out, **Paulo**: I love water sports, **Mikhael**: I'm a university student, **Stefan**: I play football, **Claudette**: I'm a ski instructor, **Maria**: I also like running.

7 Divide the class into pairs and allow students five minutes to find the best keypal for each person. Encourage them to think of reasons for their choices.

8 Write *We think (Paulo) is a good keypal for (Maria) (because) …* on the board while students are working. When the time limit is up, get students to tell the class about their choices, e.g. *We think Claudette is a good keypal for Mikhael. He's Russian and she went to Russia last year.*
Encourage other students to say why they agree or disagree, e.g. *We don't think Claudette is a good keypal for Mikhael. She's 25 and he's 20.*
There are no right and wrong answers for this matching activity.

9 Ask students *Who is a good keypal for you?* Then write the results on the board to discover who is the class's favourite keypal.

Follow up

● Set up an activity in which students become keypals (or penfriends) within their own or another class. Alternatively, students can find genuine keypals via an exchange programme or using a keypal website.

Write around the world

Do you want to practise your English? Do you want to make friends around the world! Then read about the keypals below and start writing!

Hello! My name is Belén Lopez and I'm looking for a keypal. I'm twenty-two years old and I'm from Madrid in Spain. I'm a nurse. I work long hours, but in my free time I do a lot of sport. And I like eating out with my friends. In Spain we eat very late in the evening. Write to me at Box 001.

Hi! My name is Paulo Dias and I'm Brazilian. I live in Rio de Janeiro near the sea – I love water sports! I teach music in a school. I love music too! What else? I'm twenty-four years of age and I'm single. My box number is 002.

Hello. I'm a 20-year-old Russian university student (engineering). I live with my family in Moscow. I want to write to other people around the world. My hobbies are computer games and the Internet. Please write to Box 003 to find out more. I nearly forgot – my name is Mikhael Pavlov.

I'm Stefan Zilliken and I work in a travel agent's in Munich in the south of Germany. I was 23 on January 1st. My hobbies are football – I play and I watch – and walking in the mountains. I also get some free holidays with my job! Perhaps I can come to your country! I'm at Box 004.

Hi! My name's Claudette Romand and I'm French. My home is in Lyons, but I work in Meribel – I'm a ski instructor there. I work in the winter – but in the summer I like to travel. (I went to Russia last summer.) I like photography too – so I always have a camera with me! Oh yes, I'm 25 years old. Contact me at Box 005.

I'm Maria Szopen, twenty-one years old, and I'm from Warsaw, the capital of Poland. I'm a computer programmer. In the evenings I go to the cinema – but English films are difficult for me! I also like running – I'm a member of a big athletics club. You will find me at Box 006.

name					
age	24				
nationality		Polish			
home city			Lyons		
job				travel agent	
hobbies					computer games, Internet

1.2

The numbers game

LEVEL
Intermediate

TOPIC
Names and personal characteristics

ACTIVITY TYPE
Read-and-do code-breaking

READING FOCUS
Recognising main ideas, intensive reading

TIME
30–40 minutes

KEY LANGUAGE
clever, confident, determined, friendly, happy, honest, imaginative, intelligent, kind, lazy, nice, optimistic, patient, polite, quick, quiet, reliable, sad, sensible, serious, shy, thoughtful

Present tense of *be*; present simple; comparative and superlative adjectives

PREPARATION
One photocopy for each student. You might like to read the text and work out your own number

Warm up

1   Ask students if they ever do magazine quizzes or questionnaires that allow them to find out more about themselves. Explain that they are going to read a text which will allow them to find out more about their personality.

2   Get students to suggest words to describe personality and write a list on the board. Elicit or introduce the words in Key language, which are all in the text.

Main activity

1   Give each student a photocopy. Look at the heading *The numbers game* with the class. Ask students to look quickly at the text and decide how the game works. Letters of the alphabet equal numbers, which can be used to describe personality types.

2   Tell students to read the text as far as *so Mary Brown's lucky number is three*. Make sure that they understand that they can find out what kind of person Mary is by reading the description of *threes*.

3   Write the following names on the board:

Alice King, Gareth Jones, Cathy Parker, Simon West,
Jane Lee, Alan Brown, Sally Frame, Peter Crisp, Anne Thorne.

Explain that the names on the board belong to the people in the pictures. Students follow the instructions in the text and find out each person's lucky number using the letters of their name. They then match the people with their pictures. If you like, you can tell the class that the women's names are *Alice King, Cathy Parker, Jane Lee, Sally Frame* and *Anne Thorne*.

4   Check the answers with the class. Say each name in turn and get students to call out the number. If there is any disagreement, get a volunteer student to copy the name onto the board and to work out the number as for *Mary Brown*.

Answer key		
1 Alan Brown	**4** Sally Frame	**7** Jane Lee
2 Simon West	**5** Gareth Jones	**8** Alice King
3 Peter Crisp	**6** Anne Thorne	**9** Cathy Parker

5   Get students to suggest the name of a famous person and write the person's name on the board. If you like, get students to suggest adjectives to describe this person and write a list on the board.

6   Tell students to work out the number of the person they chose. Ask them if they agree with the description of this person.

7   Ask students to work out their own number. Ask them if they agree with the description.

Follow up

●   Students write an alternative description for their own number. Tell them to describe how they would like to be, e.g. *Eights are the most thoughtful people in the world.* They can then read all the alternative descriptions for the numbers and decide which they prefer.

The numbers game

Follow these instructions and work out your lucky number. Then find this number and read about yourself. You can find out all about your friends or relatives. All you need to know is the person's name.

1	2	3	4	5	6	7	8	9
A	B	C	D	E	F	G	H	I
J	K	L	M	N	O	P	Q	R
S	T	U	V	W	X	Y	Z	

This is what you do. Write a friend's name on a piece of paper, and use the chart to find out the number for each letter.
For example:

M	A	R	Y		B	R	O	W	N
4	1	9	7		2	9	6	5	5

Now add up all the numbers.
4 + 1 + 9 + 7 + 2 + 9 + 6 + 5 + 5 = 48

Keep adding until you have just one number.
4 + 8 = 12
1 + 2 = 3

This number is your friend's lucky number, so Mary Brown's lucky number is three.

1 ONES

Ones are the most confident and determined of all the numbers. They can do anything when they want to. Ones hate people telling them what to do, but they like telling other people what to do.

2 TWOS

Twos are kind, shy, thoughtful and polite. They love animals, reading and staying at home. They usually feel really happy or sad.

3 THREES

Threes are certainly not lazy. They always do their work on time and still have lots of free time for hobbies. They're also honest, sensible, reliable and patient with other people.

4 FOURS

Fours are quick and clever, and they can make people laugh. They're not shy about saying what they think, but people don't always like what they say.

5 FIVES

Fives are quicker than most people. They're more intelligent too. They're interested in lots of different things and are very friendly. They love travel and trying new things.

6 SIXES

Sixes are the happiest and the most optimistic of all the numbers. They find something good even when things are bad. They've got lots of friends because they're so nice!

7 SEVENS

Sevens are clever, serious and quiet, and usually have only one or two close friends. They like being alone. They don't like noisy crowds and large groups of people. Sevens love animals and the countryside.

8 EIGHTS

Eights are sensible, reliable and nice. In fact, they're sometimes too kind to other people. They work hard and try hard at their hobbies.

9 NINES

Nines are clever and imaginative, but they're sometimes lazy. They like having fun, and they are fun to be with. People usually like nines a lot, but nines are not always kind to other people.

1.3

Famous last words

LEVEL
Upper-intermediate

TOPIC
What famous people
said before they died

ACTIVITY TYPE
Matching quotations
with people

**READING
FOCUS**
Text cohesion,
paraphrasing

TIME
40–50 minutes

KEY LANGUAGE
*committed suicide,
died, drowned,
hanged, killed, shot*

PREPARATION
One photocopy for
each pair of students –
cut into two parts (the
Quotations and the
Situations, with the
Situations cut into
sixteen strips)

Warm up

1 Bear in mind that death is a taboo subject and should be treated sensitively. Begin the lesson by revising and/or pre-teaching words associated with death. Ask students to explain the difference between *died* (stopped living) and *killed* (made someone die). Write the two words on the board and give students time to think of ways of dying and ways of killing. Encourage them to work together in pairs or small groups so that they can help each other.

2 Check the answers with the class. Make sure that you include the following words which are all in the text: *died: committed suicide, drowned; killed: shot, hanged.*

3 Explain to students that they are going to read and discuss some famous last words, i.e. what famous people said before they died. Ask students if they know of any examples. For example, W. Somerset Maugham, the British writer is supposed to have said, 'Dying is a very dull, dreary affair. And my advice to you is to have nothing to do with it' before he died in 1965.

Main activity

1 Give each pair of students the Quotations.

2 Discuss the first quotation with the class. Ask students to think about who might have said this before dying, not necessarily which specific person, but what kind of person and in what situation. Do not confirm or correct students' predictions at this point.

3 Ask students to work in their pairs and predict who might have said each of the things. They write their predictions in a list.

4 Give each pair of students a set of people with their situations. Tell students to match the people with the quotations.

5 Ask students to comment on how each person died and the significance of their words.

> **Suggested answers**
> 1 Oates did not come back to the tent.
> 2 Sedwick was shot dead mid-sentence by someone he thought couldn't kill an elephant.
> 3 King Albert did not join his companions in an hour. He fell to his death.
> 4 Cleopatra found the snake ('it') which then killed her.
> 5 William was shot dead by his servant.
> 6 Archimedes was more concerned with his mathematical problems than the soldiers who would kill him.
> 7 Beethoven would no longer be deaf after his death.
> 8 Mozart was writing a requiem – a piece of music for a religious ceremony at which people honour and pray for a dead person – when he died.
> 9 Elvis may have been talking about the press conference – he can't have bored people with his music!
> 10 Richard would give up his kingdom to anyone who could give him a horse so that he could escape the battle.
> 11 Houdini was always fighting – against chains, etc. – but these didn't 'get' him.
> 12 Monelete was paralysed by the bull.
> 13 Leonardo could never have been accused of low-quality work!
> 14 Marx felt that he had said enough.
> 15 Cherokee Bill just wanted to get his hanging over.

Follow up
• Discuss the quotations with the class. Which do students particularly like?

Quotations

1 I am just going outside and I may be some time.

2 They couldn't hit an elephant at this dist ...

3 If I feel in good form, I shall take the difficult way up. If I do not, I shall take the easy one. I shall join you in an hour.

4 So here it is!

5 Shoot, Walter, shoot, as if it were the devil.

6 Stand away, fellow, from my diagram!

7 I shall hear in heaven!

8 Did I not tell you I was writing this for myself?

9 I hope I have not bored you.

10 A horse, a horse, my kingdom for a horse!

11 I am tired of fighting. I guess this thing is going to get me.

12 I can't feel anything in my right leg. I can't feel anything in my left leg. Doctor, are my eyes open? I can't see.

13 I have offended God and mankind because my work did not reach the quality it should have.

14 Go on, get out! Last words are for fools who haven't said enough.

15 No. I came here to die. Not to make a speech. The quicker this thing's over the better.

Situations

Captain Lawrence Oates
British explorer, a member of Scott's ill-fated 1912 expedition to the South Pole. Said as he walked out of the tent to his death.

General Sedwick
American Civil War commander; shot at the battle of Spotsylvania. Foolishly standing up and looking at the enemy army.

Albert I
King of Belgium, killed in a climbing accident 1934. To his companions as he set off on his own route.

Cleopatra
Queen of Egypt, committed suicide 30 BC. On finding the poisonous snake in a bowl of fruit.

William II
King of England, killed in a hunting accident 1100. To his servant, who fired, but not at the deer.

Archimedes
Greek mathematician, killed 212 BC. To the invading soldiers who killed him.

Ludwig van Beethoven
German composer, deaf for the last 25 years of his life, died 1827.

Wolfgang Amadeus Mozart
Austrian composer, died 1791. Playing his own 'Requiem'.

Elvis Presley
American rock superstar, died 1977. His final press conference ended with these words.

Richard III
English king, killed at the battle of Bosworth Field, 1485. (According to Shakespeare's Richard III.)

Harry Houdini (Erich Weiss)
American magician and entertainer who had performed many amazing escapes, died 1926.

Monelete (Manuel Laureano Rodriguez Sanchez)
Spanish bullfighter, killed in the bullring 1947.

Leonardo da Vinci
Italian scientist and artist, died 1519.

Karl Marx
German philosopher and economist, died 1883. Asked by his housekeeper if he had a last message to the world.

Cherokee Bill
American criminal, hanged 1896. Asked if he had anything to say.

2.1

77 years of marriage

LEVEL
Elementary

TOPIC
Longest married
couple in Britain

ACTIVITY TYPE
Reading
comprehension

**READING
FOCUS**
Skimming for text
type and topic,
scanning for specific
words, identifying
pronoun references,
inferring information
from textual clues, text
reconstruction

TIME
40–50 minutes

KEY LANGUAGE
leave school, start work,
meet (someone),
fall in love, get engaged,
get married, have children,
retire

Past simple

PREPARATION
One photocopy for
each student – cut into two
parts (the text and the
Exercises)

Warm up

1 Write the words and phrases from Key language on the board in random order. Tell
students that they are going to read a text which includes these words. Ask what they
think the text will be about (someone's life).

2 Ask students to put the stages of life in order. When you check the order, elicit the past
tense form of the verbs.

Main activity

1 Give each student the text. Tell students that they have one minute to look at it. Then ask
a) where the text is from, b) what it is about and c) who is in the photos. Draw students'
attention to the date of the article.

> **Answer key**
> **a)** a newspaper   **b)** the longest married couple in the UK
> **c)** Fred and Olive Hodges, the longest married couple

2 Ask students to read the first paragraph and find four of the stages of life on the board.

3 Explain that newspaper articles often give the main points of the story in the first paragraph
and then return to them later in the article. Ask students in which paragraph the stages of
life are mentioned again. Then ask what paragraph 4 is about .

> **Answer key**
> **paragraph 2 (and 3)** – met (someone); **paragraph 5** – got engaged / engagement,
> got married / marriage; **paragraph 4** – the First World War.

4 Ask students to read the text again and find the other stages of life in the list on the board.

> **Answer key**
> **paragraph 2** – left school, started work; **paragraph 5** – had children;
> **paragraph 6** – retired/retirement

5 Elicit the pronouns and possessive adjectives which are used to talk about Fred (*he, him,
his*), Olive (*she, her, her*) and the couple (*they, them, their*). Ask students to find these
words in the text and to check that they all refer to Fred, Olive and the couple. Elicit that
the use of *he* and *his* in paragraph 7 refers to John, their son.

6 Ask students to find examples of *I, my, me* and *we, us, our* and decide who they refer to.
Point out that these can all be found in the direct speech, and depend on who is speaking.

> **Answer key**
> **paragraphs 3 and 6**   I, me = Olive   we, our = Olive and Fred
> **paragraph 4**   I = Fred
> **paragraphs 7 and 8**   I, my = John   us, our = John and Brenda

7 Give each student the exercises. Encourage students to work together in pairs so that they
can help each other with Exercise A. Then they complete the summary of the text for
Exercise B.

> **Answer key**
> **Exercise A**
> **1** True: The couple met ... as they skated on a frozen river.
> **2** True: The couple met ... in Northampton. ... Back home in Northampton, Fred ...
> **3** False: The couple met ... in 1915. But, three years later ... Fred joined the army.
> **4** True: Fred and Olive ... have been married for 77 years in April 2002.
> **5** True: Fred worked for the gas company in Northampton. After his marriage, Fred
>   became chief cashier at the gas company.
> **6** False: The couple now have 11 grandchildren and 12 great-grandchildren.
> **Exercise B**
> **1** met in **2** 1919 after the **3** in love and got **4** a house and got **5** had two
> **6** retired in the **7** are both **8** 11 grandchildren and 12 **9** in an old people's
> **10** married for 77 years **11** the UK's

Longest married couple celebrate 77 years of marriage

Fred and Olive Hodges, who have been married for 77 years in April, are about to enter the Guinness Book of Records as the UK's longest married couple. The couple first met in 1915, then were separated by the First World War. They met again in 1919 and fell in love. They got engaged and married – but only after six years, when they had saved £600 to buy their first house.

The couple, who are both 102, met in their teens as they skated on a frozen river in Northampton in 1915. Fred had left school at 15 and started work for the local gas company; Olive had left at 14 and worked in a leather factory.

'I wasn't really interested at the time, I just wanted to have fun on the ice,' said Olive. 'Fred came up behind me and knocked me down. He told me years later that he did it because he wanted to pick me up.'

But, three years later, when he was 18, Fred joined the army and was soon fighting in France. Many of his comrades were killed. Fred published a book of his memories, *Men of 18 in 1918*, in 1988. In his book he described how a sudden silence signalled that war was over. 'Now I knew I was going to have a life after all.'

Back home in Northampton, Fred renewed his friendship with Olive. The couple had a six-year engagement before their marriage. They had two children, John and Brenda. Fred became chief cashier at the gas company. Olive stayed at home while the children grew up. The couple now have 11 grandchildren and 12 great-grandchildren – the latest just two years old. Two years ago they had to leave their own home because of Fred's poor health. They now live together in an old people's home in Wellsborough, Leicestershire.

'We have lots of lovely memories but the birth of our two children is the most special,' said Olive. And the best decade for me was when Fred retired in the 1960s. His retirement just meant we could spend more time together. I love Fred so much. I don't know what I would do without him.'

Their son, John, 73, a retired professor of genetics who lives in Austria, is full of praise for his parents. 'They are completely devoted to each other,' he said. 'And my sister and I could not have more loving parents.'

The couple yesterday

© Caters News

'My mother gave up her life for her family and home. Our parents opened doors of opportunity for us which they never had themselves and encouraged us to go through them.'

Fred and Olive on their wedding day

© Caters News

✂ -

Exercise A

The sentences below are not in the text. Use other information in the text to decide if the sentences are true or false. What information helped you?

1 Fred and Olive first met in winter.

2 They were from Northampton.

3 Fred joined the army in 1915.

4 They got married in April 1925.

5 They bought a house in Northampton.

6 John and Brenda didn't have children.

Exercise B

Complete the sentences and write a summary of the newspaper article.

Fred and Olive first .¹. 1915. They met again in .². war. They fell .³. engaged. In 1925 they bought .⁴. married. Fred and Olive .⁵. children. Fred .⁶. 1960s.

The couple .⁷. 102. They now have .⁸. great-grandchildren. They live .⁹. home. They have been .¹⁰. in April. They are .¹¹. longest married couple.

2.2

What's the best age to get married?

LEVEL
Intermediate

TOPIC
Marriage and the best age to do it

ACTIVITY TYPE
Note-taking

READING FOCUS
Scanning for names, reading for detail, separating fact and opinion

TIME
40–50 minutes

KEY LANGUAGE
Present simple; past simple

PREPARATION
One photocopy for each pair of students – cut into three parts (the texts, Exercise A, and Exercise B)

Warm up

1 Explain to students that they are going to read about and discuss the best age to get married. Ask the class how many students are married. How long have they been married? Ask the unmarried students if they would like to get married. When?

Main activity

1 Divide the class into pairs. Gve each pair of students the texts. Allow students one minute to find the names of the five speakers and their partners.

2 Check the answers with the class. Write the names on the board. (See Answer key below.)

3 Give each pair of students Exercise A. Add columns 1–4 to the chart on the board. Make sure that students understand how the exercise works.

4 Tell students to copy the chart on the board. They then read the texts and complete the chart with information about each speaker.

5 Check the answers with the class and complete the chart on the board. Encourage students to find evidence for their answers in the text. For Paula, for example, *1 James and I got married, 2 when I was 35, 3 I only met James three years ago. It's a pity we didn't meet sooner.*

Answer key

	1	2	3	4
Paula Dawson + James	yes	no	no	—
Victoria Kidman + Richard	yes	yes	yes	—
Jill Boston + William	yes	yes	no	—
Katie Lee + Dan	yes	no	yes	—
Amanda Brown + Tom	no	—	—	no

6 Give each pair of students Exercise B. Explain that each of the six statements refers to one of the speakers. Go through an example with the class. Elicit that *She comes from Birmingham* refers to Katie.

7 Ask students to continue to work in pairs. They decide who each statement refers to.

8 Check the answers with the class. Then ask students if the statements describe facts or opinions.

Answer key
1 Katie (fact)   **2** Amanda (fact)   **3** Jill (fact)
4 Victoria (opinion)   **5** Paula (opinion)   **6** Katie (opinion)

9 Allow students time to read each profile again. Tell them to underline facts with blue pen. Make sure that everyone agrees that most of the information expresses the speakers' opinions, although sometimes there is an overlap between fact and opinion. For example, did Victoria's friends have ups and downs in their relationships, or is that simply Victoria's opinion?

Answer key
Paula – got married when she was 35, a yoga instructor from Bristol, she only met James three years ago
Victoria – her parents are divorced, a teacher who married her partner, Richard, when they were both 23, Richard's parents were quite old when he was born
Jill – 38, married at 24, now in the process of getting divorced, had two children
Katie – got married when she was 28, a 33-year-old computer programmer from Birmingham, married to Dan
Amanda – in her mid-thirties, been with her partner for more than ten years, has three children, has talked about getting married, she and Tom love each other, Tom's brothers are divorced

'James and I got married when I was 35,' says Paula Dawson, a yoga instructor from Bristol. 'I wanted to get married when I was younger, but I didn't meet the right person when I was in my twenties. I only met James three years ago. It's a pity we didn't meet sooner, because we're perfect for each other. We have so much in common, as well as our own individual interests, which I think is important. The big problem now is: will I be able to have children? If you get married in your twenties and find out that there are problems, you have more time to sort them out. I'm just keeping my fingers crossed at the moment.'

'My parents are divorced, so I suppose I wanted security,' says Victoria Kidman, a teacher who married her partner, Richard, when they were both 23. 'Also, Richard's parents were quite old when he was born, and he wants to be a father when he's still young. I felt we'd made an important statement – that we wanted to spend the rest of our lives together. Since we got married, lots of our friends have had relationship ups and downs, and I'm just glad we made a commitment when we were young and didn't have those problems. Getting married after knowing each other for just two years meant we still had things to discover about each other. Getting to know each other as a married couple made it very special.'

'Twenty-four is just too young,' says Jill Boston, 38, who married at that age but is now in the process of getting divorced from her husband. 'You haven't had enough experience of life to really appreciate the person you're with. William felt he'd missed out at work, because he had two small children, and I felt I'd missed out on that carefree, irresponsible attitude you're only allowed to have in your 20s. Even though getting married young was the ultimate proof of commitment, and I appreciate being a relatively young mum, your 20s are your only chance for putting yourself first.'

'I read recently that the average first-time bride is 28, while her groom is 30. I got married when I was 28, and I'm pleased I waited until then,' says Katie Lee, a 33-year-old computer programmer from Birmingham who is married to Dan. 'In your early 20s, you're not an independent person. If you stay single until your late 20s, you've developed as a full individual. If you get together in your early 20s, you don't have time to develop your own individuality. Instead, you have a joint identity with your partner. Other people see you as a couple, and outside that couple identity you have to work out who you are. In addition, if you wait until you're older before getting married, you have a better idea of the kind of person you want to marry.'

'It's estimated that one third of couples in Britain will be unmarried by the year 2021,' says Amanda Brown. 'And my partner Tom and I will be one of those couples. We're both in our mid-thirties now, and we've been together more than ten years. We have three children, too. Tom and I have talked about getting married, but we don't see why we should. We know we love each other, so what do we have to prove to the world? Plus the fact that both Tom's brothers are divorced – that has rather put him off marriage. Also, of course, getting married takes a lot of organisation – the ceremony, a party, the clothes. No, thank you. It's not for me!'

Exercise A

1   Is she married?
    If the answer is **yes**, go on to question 2.
    If the answer is **no**, go on to question 4.

2   Did she get married young?
    If the answer is **yes** or **no**, go on to question 3.

3   Is she happy that she got married when she did?
    If the answer is **yes** or **no**, go on to the next person.

4   Does she want to get married?
    If the answer is **yes** or **no**, go on to the next person.

Exercise B

1   She comes from Birmingham.

2   She has three children.

3   She got married when she was 24.

4   She's pleased she and her husband married when they were young.

5   She thinks getting married younger is better for you if you want to have children.

6   She thinks you don't know what kind of person you want to marry if you're young when you get married.

2.3

Is that fur comment?

LEVEL
Upper-intermediate

TOPIC
The British and their pets

ACTIVITY TYPE
Identifying idioms in a text, working out their meaning

READING FOCUS
Deducing meaning from context

TIME
40–50 minutes

KEY LANGUAGE
animal idioms

PREPARATION
One photocopy for each student – cut into three parts (the paraphrases cut into fifteen strips, the text and the Exercise)

Warm up

1 Explain to students that they are going to work with some English idioms. Explain that an idiom is an expression whose meaning is not obvious from the individual words. For example, *the apple of someone's eye* means *the person who someone loves most and is very proud of*, but we cannot know this by looking at the individual words. The best way to understand an idiom is from its context. It should be possible to work out the meaning of *the apple of someone's eye* from this context: *Pete's daughter was the apple of his eye. He adored her and she could do no wrong.* Encourage students to tell the class any English idioms that they know.

2 Explain to students that they are going to read an article about the British and their pets. Ask what pets they think the British have.

3 Read out the title of the article. Explain that the use of *fur* in the question plays on the question *Is that fair comment?*, which means *Is that a reasonable thing to say?* Read out the bi-line below the title. Explain that the writer feels that animals are portrayed negatively in English idioms.

Main activity

1 Give each student the text. Tell students to raise their hand as soon as they know which pet the writer has.

2 Ask students to find the idiom in the first paragraph. Then ask them to work out the meaning of the idiom from its context and paraphrase it in everyday English.

> **Answer key**
> **1** The writer has dogs.
> **2** It's a dog's life = idiom.
> Life is hard and unpleasant = paraphrase.

3 Tell students to read the texts, and find and underline 14 further idioms which they should then try and paraphrase. Encourage students to work together in pairs or small groups so that they can help each other. Particularly if students are struggling, point out that the idioms are all within double quotes, although not everything in double quotes is an idiom.

4 Check that students have found all 15 idioms. Get individual students to read out an idiom each. Do not check paraphrases at this point. Instead give each student a set of paraphrases. Ask students to match the idioms with the paraphrases.

5 Check the answers with the class. Read out the idioms in the order in which they appear in the text. Get individual students to read out the corresponding definition. The paraphrases on the worksheet are in the correct order.

6 Give each student the Exercise. Students complete the sentences with the idioms.

> **Answer key**
> **1** dog's breakfast
> **2** dog
> **3** it's a dog's life
> **4** gone to the dogs
> **5** in the doghouse
> **6** It's raining cats and dogs
> **7** the cat that got the cream
> **8** There's more than one way to skin a cat
> **9** There's not enough room to swing a cat
> **10** the cat's whiskers
> **11** let the cat out of the bag
> **12** as sick as a dog
> **13** while the cat's away, the mice will play
> **14** Love me, love my dog
> **15** a pig in a poke

Follow up

• Students write personalised sentences using the idioms. Point out that it is more important, however, for them to recognise the meaning of an idiom than to be able to use it themselves.

Is that fur comment?

The British may be a nation of animal lovers, but the way our language treats our four-legged friends is not something to be proud of, argues **Justine Hankins**

The other day, I was thinking about the phrase "It's a dog's life". According to my dictionary, this means "life is hard and unpleasant", but that definition is surely obsolete. A dog's life these days, at least in my house, means one of pampered leisure.

This is by no means the only phrase in the English language that suggests a dog's life is a miserable one. When we become less successful than we were in the past, we "go to the dogs"; when we do something very badly, we make a "dog's breakfast" of it; if we feel really bad, we're "as sick as a dog". Unattractive or unpleasant people are considered canine in appearance, as in "Ugh, how could you? He's such a dog!" And those who have irritated or offended us and caused our disapproval are sent to "the doghouse".

Cats do no better. They are proverbially portrayed as humourless tyrants ("While the cat's away, the mouse will play") or as self-satisfied and smug ("The cat that got the cream"). They are also subjected to unspeakable horrors in many of the phrases that we still use in everyday speech. The origin of the charming phrase "There's more than one way to skin a cat" is lost in the mists of time, but the equally frightful "There's not enough room to swing a cat" in all likelihood doesn't refer to a cat at all. "Cat" is an abbreviation for the cat-o'-nine-tails, a rope whip with nine knotted thongs and the phrase probably originated at sea, where unfortunate sailors were flogged in confined spaces. One consolation is that "the cat's whiskers" are the most desirable whiskers.

How our domesticated companions entered the language in this way is often shrouded in mystery, but there are some examples that reference book writers will try to explain. "To let the cat out of the bag" probably refers to dodgy fairground traders who tried to pass off an inedible old cat as a nice juicy piglet, and is possibly a close cousin of "pig in a poke". "It's raining cats and dogs", meanwhile, is often poetically explained as a reference to Norse mythology, which associated cats with the mystical force controlling the weather and dogs with the wind. Other sources suggest that it dates from the time when inner-city gutters overflowed with rubbish, sewage and dead animals.

Many of these phrases reflect a time when cats and dogs were not as cherished as they are now. My own personal motto "love me, love my dog" dates back as far as 1485, when it was recorded in a book called Early English Miscellanies. Although originally the implication of this may have been "If you really love me, you will have to accept my boils and pox scars", it now means "If you love me, you will get to play with my gorgeous little doggies, too".

Paraphrases

something you say which means that life is hard and unpleasant

a country or organisation is becoming less successful than it was in the past

something that has been done very badly (informal)

to be very sick

a man who is unpleasant or not to be trusted, or an unattractive woman

someone is annoyed with another person because of something they have done (informal)

something you say which means when the person in authority is absent, people will not do what they should do

someone annoys other people by looking very pleased with themselves because of something good that they have done

something you say which means that there are several possible ways of achieving something (humorous)

something you say to describe a place that is very small (informal)

to be extremely good

to tell people secret information, often without intending to

something you buy or accept without first seeing it or knowing what it is like, with the result that it might not be what you want

something you say when it is raining very heavily (old-fashioned)

means that if you really love someone, you will have to accept everything about them (saying)

Exercise

1 You should have seen the dress after I ironed it. It was a complete … .

2 I don't like Jim at all. He's a real … .

3 I've got to do my homework, tidy my bedroom, then help my dad – … .

4 Some workers say that this company has … .

5 I forgot to post a letter for my sister, so I'm really … .

6 There's water running down the street. … out there!

7 Kelly got top marks in the exam, so she was looking like … .

8 You can pay by cheque, credit card or cash. …, you know.

9 … in my office. It's tiny!

10 She thought she was … with her new haircut.

11 I was trying to keep my age a secret, but my son went and … .

12 He was … after the meal. I don't know what he'd eaten.

13 Your boss might regret taking such a long holiday. You know, … .

14 Sonia's new boyfriend doesn't like children, and she's got three. '…', as they say.

15 Booking a hotel over the phone is … . You don't know what kind of room you will get.

3.1

Where did I see you?

LEVEL
Elementary

TOPIC
What happened
last week

ACTIVITY TYPE
Problem-solving
through groupwork
question-and-
answer, role play

**READING
FOCUS**
Extracting key
information

TIME
40–50 minutes

KEY LANGUAGE
Past simple, regular
and irregular verbs

PREPARATION
One photocopy for
each group of four
students – cut into four
parts

Warm up

1   Ask students what they did at the weekend. Make sure that they use the past simple correctly. Encourage them to ask questions, e.g. *What did you do on Saturday? Did you go to the cinema on Friday?*

2   Explain to students that they are going to take part in a role play in which they talk about what they did last week. They are going to work in groups of four, with a diary each. They imagine they are one of the four diary writers and they must ask questions to find out which other person did the same thing at the same time as themselves.

Main activity

1   Divide the class into groups of four. Give each student in the group a different diary.

2   Draw the following chart on the board and tell students to copy it. They then read their diary and complete the column *me* with the activity they did. Point out that it is not necessary to understand every word in the diary, just the main points.

	me	the others
Monday		
Tuesday		
Wednesday		
Thursday		
Friday		
Saturday		

3   Ask students to work in pairs within their group. They take it in turns to ask each other questions until they find out on which evening their partner did the same activity as they did. They then write this person's name next to the activity in the column *the others*. For example, Sam writes *Pat* in the top row of her chart because they both went to a restaurant.

4   Tell students to work with all three group members and complete their chart.

5   Check the answers with the class. Encourage students to talk about when they did what other people did, e.g. *I'm Sam. On Monday Pat and I went to a restaurant. On Friday Jo and I went to the tennis club.*

6   Tell students to find out a) the evening when none of the four people did the same thing, and b) the evening when everyone did the same as one other person.

7   Check the answers with the class.

> **Answer key**
> **a)** On Wednesday none of the four people did the same thing.
> **b)** On Saturday each person did the same thing as one other.
>
> | | Sam | Jo | Pat | Chris |
> |---|---|---|---|---|
> | Monday | **restaurant** | **swimming pool** | **restaurant** | **tennis club** |
> | Tuesday | doctor's | football match | **cinema** | **cinema** |
> | Wednesday | home | **restaurant** | art class | doctor's |
> | Thursday | **cinema** | **museum** | **swimming pool** | **museum** |
> | Friday | **tennis club** | **tennis club** | **party** | wine bar |
> | Saturday | **party** | **theatre** | **theatre** | **party** |

Follow up

•   Students copy the chart again. They complete the column *me* with six different (imaginary) activities. They then ask questions to find out what other students did and write in *the others* column the name of any student who did the same activity.

Sam

Monday

I went to San Marco's with some people from work. I love Italian food!

Tuesday

I didn't feel well, so I went to the doctor's after work. Perhaps it was something I ate last night?

Wednesday

I didn't go to work. I didn't feel well, so I stayed at home all day.

Thursday

I didn't feel great, but I decided to go to the cinema. I saw an awful film in Spanish.

Friday

I played tennis at the club with three friends. Mel and I didn't win!

Saturday

I went to a party at my neighbour Paul's house with Mel. We had a great time!

Pat

Monday

I went to the new Italian restaurant with Mum and Dad. Very nice!

Tuesday

In the evening, I went to the cinema with my sister. We saw the latest Bond film.

Wednesday

I went to my art class after work. Unfortunately, my painting isn't getting any better.

Thursday

I went swimming with Rob. We swam fifty lengths – and talked all the time!

Friday

One of my colleagues was having a party. I stayed for an hour, then I went home.

Saturday

I went to the theatre with some people from work. I love Shakespeare!

Jo

Monday

I went to the swimming pool after work. I didn't stay long – the water was really cold!

Tuesday

I watched a football match – I don't like football, but my brother was playing!

Wednesday

I went to the Italian restaurant that opened last month. I had some delicious spaghetti!

Thursday

It was late-night opening at the museum, so I went for an hour after work.

Friday

I went to the tennis club after work. I played really badly!

Saturday

Ashley had some tickets for Romeo and Juliet. I fell asleep in the middle!

Chris

Monday

I played tennis for a couple of hours at the club. Then it started to rain.

Tuesday

Kim and I went to the cinema after work. James Bond films are our favourite!

Wednesday

I had to go to the doctor's after work. I needed some injections before my holiday.

Thursday

I went to the Japanese exhibition at the museum after work. I loved the kimonos.

Friday

Some of my colleagues were going to a wine bar, so I went with them. I didn't stay long.

Saturday

I went to my friend Paul's party in the evening. There were lots of people there!

3.2

LEVEL
Intermediate

TOPIC
Cooking

ACTIVITY TYPE
Note-taking

READING FOCUS
Skimming to identify topic, recognising main ideas, reading 'between the lines'

TIME
40–50 minutes

KEY LANGUAGE
dish, equipment, grill, ingredients, pan, oven, recipe

PREPARATION
One photocopy for each group of three students – cut into six parts (the texts and the photos)

Men who cook

Warm up

1 Explain that you are going to discuss some words from the text. Deal with the words in Key language. Write the word *dish* on the board. Explain that a *dish* is both a shallow container for food and a type of food prepared in a particular way. Give examples of a dish, e.g. *paella, beef stroganoff*. Then give examples of *ingredients* for these dishes. Continue with the *equipment*, e.g. a *pan*, and then talk about where you would cook the dish.

Main activity

1 Give each group of three students the texts. Ask them to check the topic of the text. Tell them that these texts are based on an article from a British cookery magazine.

2 Ask students to read the texts and work out if the writers are men or women. Encourage students to look at one text each.

3 Discuss the answers with the class, but do not confirm whether students' answers are correct.

> **Answer key**
> All three speakers are men: top, *my wife*; middle, *women like the fact that I cook, my girlfriend, the real reason why boys like cooking*; bottom, no clues.

4 Give each group of students the three photos. Ask them to match the photos with the texts. Get them to suggest a title for the magazine article.

5 Make statements about each writer, e.g. a) *He lived in a flat last year*; b) *He bought himself a special pan to cook his speciality*; c) *He talks to his wife while he's cooking* Ask students to raise their hand if the statement is about the writer of their text.

> **Answer key**
> **a)** Christopher   **b)** Alex   **c)** Andrew

6 Write the questions in the chart in Answer key below on the board.

7 Tell students to copy the questions and complete a chart about the three men. Again, encourage them to look at one text each, but to show their partners the information they have found. Students who are looking at the same text can work together, and then report back to their group. Point out that each writer may not answer all the questions; students should read 'between the lines' and suggest their probable answer.

8 Check the answers with the class. Get individual students to answer a question each.

> **Answer key**

	Andrew	Christopher	Alex
When and why did he start cooking?	when a student with not enough money to eat out	doesn't say	mum taught him basics when ten; at university because tired of pasta
Who does he cook for? Are these people happy about this?	wife, who loves food	other people; last year always cooked for six students in flat – had one dish a lot, so must have liked it	friends and mum; also for girlfriend – she may not be totally happy (good cook, but rarely gets chance to cook for him)
When does he cook?	does all the cooking (probably every day)	doesn't say	at weekends and lives off that during the week
Why does he like cooking?	loves feeling of achievement; feels comfortable in kitchen	loves process of cooking – it's fun and helps him to relax; likes sociable aspect of cooking	likes equipment; relaxing; likes putting recipes together
What does he say about his cooking in the future?	starting to experiment and create own dishes	plans to go to chef school and have own café	doesn't say
What is his favourite dish or speciality?	risotto	fresh tuna, with chilli and coconut sauce	coq au vin

Follow up

- Tell students to imagine that the writers have invited them to eat their specialities. Which dish/meal would they choose? Why?

- Students work in groups, and plan starters and desserts to accompany the specialities. Students from the other groups then decide which meal they would prefer. Remember the students not the writers will cook this meal!

'I often perform four or five nights a week in concerts. Gwenda, my wife, is a great concert-goer, so we tend to eat when we get home, between 10 and 11pm. That's not ideal for digestion, so we try to eat lightly.'

'I do all the cooking. Gwenda loves food, so I like cooking for her. I'm happy with this arrangement. If I do the cooking, she does the washing up. I like preparing dinner parties for friends too.'

'I started cooking when I was a student because I didn't have enough money to eat out. I taught myself to cook using books. Until recently I always used recipes. Now, I'm starting to experiment and create my own dishes.'

'We own a VW Camper van and when my concert tours take me out of London, we spend the weekend in it. There's no oven, but it's amazing what you can do with two burners and a grill.'

'My favourite dish is risotto. It's really relaxing because you have to stir all the time. The rice takes half an hour to cook; I have a drink while I'm doing it, and my wife and I talk while I'm stirring.'

'I love the feeling of achievement that you get from cooking. I feel comfortable in the kitchen and cooking is great after the stress of work.'

© Nicky Johnston / Sainsburys magazine
New Crane Publishing Ltd

Andrew Sippings, 48, plays the viola for and is chairman of the Royal Philharmonic Orchestra. He even cooks when he's on tour.

'When I was 10, my mother, who is an amazing cook, taught me the basics. Then I cooked throughout university, mainly because I got tired of pasta.'

'I tend to cook at weekends, when I have lots of time, and then live off that during the week. Cooking should be relaxing, and I like taking a long time to cook things.'

'I have lots of recipe books by my bed and I love reading them. I tend to read lots of recipes and put them together. Following a recipe word for word is not relaxing. My speciality is coq au vin, and my own recipe comes from reading three cookery books.'

'Women like the fact that I cook until they find out that I'm a perfectionist. My girlfriend cooks very well, but she rarely gets a chance to cook for me. I like cooking for friends and I cook for my mum too. But the real reason that boys like cooking is because they like all the gadgets. Any man that disagrees is lying! When I first started making coq au vin, I bought myself a heavy-bottomed pan to cook the chicken. It's nice to have the right equipment.'

© Nicky Johnston / Sainsburys magazine
New Crane Publishing Ltd

Alex Hope, 32, is a visual-effects producer in London. His bedtime reading is usually a cookery book.

'My dad is a great cook. He has his own recipes from when he used to cook in a pub he managed with Mum. He just throws ingredients together, sees how it turns out, and it's usually delicious. We often cook together and he is very encouraging. I tend to make things up too, but use recipe books for dishes I haven't tried before.'

'I love the process of cooking. It's great fun and helps you to relax. And I like the sociable aspect of cooking for other people. Last year my cooking improved enormously because I lived in a flat with six other students. I cooked every day – lunch and dinner – and everyone else ate it. Our favourite meal was fresh tuna, with chilli and coconut sauce. We had that a lot.'

'I plan to become a chef and then open my own place. I grew up in Switzerland and there is a café there I'd like to model it on. Next year I'm getting a flat with a friend who likes cooking too, so we'll have to choose our kitchen carefully.'

© Nicky Johnston / Sainsburys magazine
New Crane Publishing Ltd

Christopher Sinclair, 23, is a biology student at Christ Church College, Oxford. He plans to go to chef school and have his own café.

3.3

Snail mail

LEVEL
Upper-intermediate

TOPIC
Snails' addiction to
saliva

ACTIVITY TYPE
Understanding
an authentic
newspaper article

**READING
FOCUS**
Deducing meaning,
inference,
summarising

TIME
40–50 minutes

KEY LANGUAGE
*culinary delicacy,
delphinium,
draught excluder,
drawback, foliage, licked,
pillar box, saliva, seal,
slime, snail, stamps,
tentacles, tickled*

PREPARATION
One photocopy for
each student – cut into
three parts (the
wordcards cut into
strips, the text and the
summary); an unused
envelope, which is
addressed but not
sealed, and a stamp

Warm up

1 Explain to students that they are going to read an article from the British newspaper *The Guardian*. The article has not been simplified in any way. In order to improve their reading and not to slow it down by constant reference to a dictionary, they need to be able to try and work out the meaning of any unknown words. This will not always be the exact meaning, but a probable or general meaning.

2 Draw a snail on the board. Get students to name the animal and to say what they know about it, e.g. *soft body, shell, tentacles, no legs, slow, leaves trails of slime*. Write the word *snail* on the board. Then add *mail* and ask students what this means.

> **Answer key**
> *Snail mail* means traditional slow post as opposed to fast e-mail.

Main activity

1 Give each student the article. Tell students to read the first paragraph and decide if the article is about snails or about snail mail, or about both.

> **Answer key**
> It is about both snails and snail mail.

2 Use the envelope to clarify the meaning of *saliva, animal glue* and *seal*.

3 Discuss any unknown words in the rest of the first paragraph with the class. Ask:
a) *What is another word for 'pillar boxes'?*
b) *What is another word for 'slimy creatures'?*
c) *What have the snails been doing to the post?*

> **Answer key**
> **a)** postboxes **b)** snails **c)** munching = eating [general]

4 Discuss the meaning of the first paragraph with the class. Ask: *What problem has the common snail been causing?* Students paraphrase the first paragraph.

5 Explain to students that they are going to read the rest of the article and find out if the problem was solved. If yes, how was it solved? If not, why not?

6 Give each student a set of wordcards. Tell students to continue reading and to consider the questions for any word that they do not understand. Tell them not to use dictionaries.

7 Divide the class into pairs. Ask students in their pairs to discuss the words on the wordcards and help each other with their meaning. Encourage them to ask similar questions about any other unknown words in the article.

8 Discuss with the class how the problem was solved, and what other problem this has created.

9 Discuss students' understanding of the words on the wordcards.

10 Point out that the article also contains references to Britain. Ask the following questions:
a) *Where is Devon and Cornwall?*   c) *What is on all British stamps?*
b) *Where is Truro?*   d) *Do British people like snails?*

> **Answer key**
> **a)** south-west **b)** south-west **c)** the Queen's image **d)** no

Follow up

● Discuss the organisation of the article with the class. Make sure that everyone agrees that the main points are in the first, third and final paragraphs, and that the important words to understand on the wordcards were *licked, draught excluders* and *drawback*.

● Tell students to summarise the article in 50 words.

● Give each student the summary. Ask students to compare their version with it. Did they include anything in their version which the summary didn't mention? Did they forget to mention anything that the summary included?

Lurking inside the postbox: snail mail

The common snail has become addicted to British saliva and the animal glue used to seal envelopes. All over Britain, it seems, slimy creatures have been crawling up pillar boxes,
5 climbing through the hole and dropping several feet into the pile of letters where they have been munching through the post in great snail feasts.

The problem was first noted in Devon and Cornwall, especially in postboxes set in stone
10 walls and surrounded by foliage. "We were finding 20, even 30 snails, at a time in the bottom of boxes," said Tom Potts, the man in charge of boxes in the south-west. 'It wasn't just ones or twos. They were leaving their slime
15 everywhere, getting into the letters, licking the paste. But they left the stamps alone, very respectful of the Queen's image.'

But the Post Office thinks it has got the snail mail phenomenon licked. Tony Gilbert, a Truro
20 postman, came up with the idea of fitting draught excluders to postboxes. The snails, it seems, do not like having their stomachs tickled by the plastic bristles.

Hundreds of boxes around Britain have been
25 fitted with excluders. 'People have been phoning from everywhere, saying "What can we do about them?" ', said Mr Potts.

The British, who tend not to view snails as a culinary delicacy, also have a particular dislike
30 of the creatures because they target prize delphiniums and vegetable gardens.

But their value is at last being recognised: scientists are trying to adapt hundreds of poisons from some snails into drugs to combat
35 pain, epilepsy, depression and schizophrenia.

The draught excluder solution has had one drawback, however. Installing them has cut off a source of income to the Post Office and its parent company, Consignia. 'We used to put the
40 [damaged] envelopes in a plastic bag and then surcharge the addressee,' said Mark Lunnen, the Devon collections planning manager.

---

foliage (line 10)

Noun, verb or adjective?

Where do snails usually live? What do they usually eat? Can you sometimes find this around postboxes?

---

licked (line 19)

Noun, verb or adjective?

Note that 'lick' here has an idiomatic meaning. It has been used because of its connection with the topic of the article, but has nothing to do with sealing envelopes. Read on and find out if the Post Office has solved its problem. What does 'licked' mean?

---

draught excluders (line 21)

Noun, verb or adjective? What is the opposite of 'exclude'?

Where exactly are the snails entering the postboxes? How could you stop snails getting in, but still allow people to post their letters? Something with 'plastic bristles'? Something you put on the bottom of a door when cold air (a 'draught') is getting in?

---

tickled (line 22)

Noun, verb or adjective?

What happens when you run a feather across the back of your hand? What is the feeling?

---

culinary delicacy (line 29)

Which word is an adjective? Which is a noun?

What do people in other countries, e.g. France, do with snails? Do the British do this?

---

delphiniums (line 31)

Noun, verb or adjective? 'Prize' is usually a noun, but is it here?

What do snails eat (or 'target')? What type of thing do they eat that might win prizes?

---

combat / epilepsy, depression and schizophrenia (lines 34–35)

Why do we use 'drugs' with 'pain'? You may not understand exactly what 'epilepsy, depression and schizophrenia' are, but what type of thing are they?

---

drawback (line 37)

Noun, verb or adjective?

Read on and work out if 'drawback' means 'advantage' or 'disadvantage'.

Summary

Snails climb into postboxes. They lick the saliva and glue on envelopes, and destroy them. The Post Office have fitted draught excluders to keep the snails out. The disadvantage of this is that the Post Office can't charge people for putting their damaged letters into plastic bags.

4.1

Room to let

LEVEL
Elementary

TOPIC
Accommodation for
language students

ACTIVITY TYPE
Matching
people with
appropriate
accommodation

**READING
FOCUS**
Reading for detail

TIME
40–50 minutes

KEY LANGUAGE
Present simple

PREPARATION
One photocopy for
each pair of students –
cut into seven parts
(the list of
Advertisements and
the six Profiles)

Warm up

1 Explain to students that they are going to read and discuss some accommodation advertisements.

2 If you are teaching in an English-speaking location, invite individual students to talk about their own accommodation. If you aren't teaching in an English-speaking location, remind students that they will need to find accommodation if they go abroad to study English or work.

Main activity

1 Give each pair of students the list of Advertisements

2 Draw the chart from Answer key below on the board. Write the questions and the letters in the chart. Work through an example with the class. For advertisement A, elicit that if a sixth person is wanted, five people already live there. Encourage students to guess the meaning of a) *mixed* and b) *bills*.

> **Answer key**
> **a)** male and female   **b)** cost of electricity, gas

3 Tell students to copy and complete the chart. Remind them that it is not necessary to understand every word in the advertisements, they only have to find the information needed to carry out the task.

4 Check the answers with the class. Encourage students to justify their answers and use this as an opportunity to clarify the meaning of any unknown vocabulary.

Answer key

	How many people already live there?	How much does it cost monthly?
A	5	£275 + bills
B	3	free
C	3	£400.00 (£100 per week) + bills
D	1	£350.00
E	0	£600.00 + bills
F	2	£350.00

5 Explain to students that they are now going to read profiles of six people who are going to Cambridge to study English for three months. They have to match each person with the most suitable accommodation.

6 Give each pair of students a set of Profiles. Set a time limit, e.g. ten minutes, for the matching.

7 Write *We think accommodation (A) is good for (Christophe) because …* on the board while students are working. When the time limit is up, get students to tell the class about their choices, e.g. *We think accommodation A is good for Christophe because the house has got parking space and he's got a car.* Encourage other students to say why they agree or disagree. There are no right and wrong answers for this matching activity, but on the worksheet the people are probably next to the most suitable accommodation.

Follow up

• Encourage students to look for accommodation advertisements in English-language newspapers. Get students to talk about which accommodation they would and wouldn't like to live in. Ask them to bring to the next class the best advertisement for their needs.

Profiles

Advertisements

A Wanted: sixth person to share mixed house. Own bedroom, share kitchen, bathroom and garden. Parking space available. Only £275 per month + bills.

B Single parent offers free accommodation in exchange for four hours a day childcare (James, 6, Helen, 8). Hours: 8.30 am – 9.30 am, 3.00 pm – 6.00 pm. Non-smoker. Weekends free.

C Share city-centre 3rd-floor flat with three foreign students. £100 per week, plus electricity. Ideally located for shops, restaurants, railway and bus station.

D *House-sit for three months while owner is away in Turkey. Cheap rent in return for answering phone and gardening. Would suit couple. £350.00 pcm, all inclusive.*

E Bedsit available from end June. Bedroom-cum-living room, plus kitchen facilities, toilet and shower. Basement, easy access to street. £600 per month + bills.

F Cat lover wanted to share house with young married couple and two cats. Six miles from city centre. Transport needed. £350 inclusive per calendar month.

Christophe Pires is 21 years old and from France. He has driven to Cambridge from his home in Lyons, and plans to drive back there twice a month to see his family and friends. Christophe doesn't like children or animals. He loves meeting new people and making new friends.

Ekatarina Mostovoi is 18 years old and from Russia. She has just left school and this is her first time abroad. Ekatarina doesn't have much money, so she is looking for a very cheap room. She wants to train as a nurse when she goes back to Moscow.

Roberto Costa is a 28-year-old engineer from São Paulo, Brazil. He travels a lot for his job, so English is important to him. This year he has been to Egypt, Turkey and Germany. Roberto doesn't like cooking, so he probably won't spend much time in the kitchen. He wants to visit lots of places while he's in England.

Tomasz Karwan is 23 years old and comes from Poland. His English is already very good, and he hopes to become an English teacher. Tomasz loves plants and animals, and being outdoors. His girlfriend, who also wants to teach English, may come and stay with him in Cambridge.

Dorothea Kahn is a 25-year-old law student from Stuttgart, Germany. Dorothea is in England to improve her English. She also wants to prepare for her law exams while she is here. She doesn't plan to go out much while she's in Cambridge. She will probably spend most evenings at her desk.

Carmen Morientes is an elementary student of English. She is very keen to improve her English and would like to live with an English family. Carmen is 22 years old, and loves animals. She is also very keen on sport. She goes running three times a week, and cycling at the weekends. She comes from Andalucia in southern Spain.

4.2

How do you explain that?

LEVEL
Intermediate

TOPIC
Urban myths connected with the home

ACTIVITY TYPE
Reading about a situation and suggesting an explanation

READING FOCUS
Extracting key information, predicting storyline

TIME
40–50 minutes

KEY LANGUAGE
Past simple

PREPARATION
One photocopy for each pair of students – cut into two parts (the Situations and the Explanations)

Warm up

1 Explain to students that they are going to read and discuss four urban myths connected with the home. Explain that an urban myth is a story that is heard and repeated until nobody knows if it is true or not.

2 Ask students if they know any urban myths, particularly any urban myths connected with the home. Encourage students to tell the class any myths they know.

Main activity

1 Give each pair of students the Situations.

2 Students work in their pairs and read each situation in turn. They then discuss an explanation for the situation and write a short ending to the story.

3 Discuss students' explanations with the class. Get individual students to read out their pair's explanation. Encourage other students to comment on the likelihood of the explanation.

4 Give each pair of students the Explanations. Tell the students to read the explanations and compare them with their own.

5 Discuss the explanations with the class. Find out which pair's explanation is closest to the explanation given.

6 Ask students to continue working in their pairs and to choose a title for each story.

7 Discuss students' titles with the class. Get students to vote for the best title for each story. If you mention the titles below, elicit or explain that if someone is *eagle-eyed*, they notice everything, even small details.

> **Suggested titles**
> **1** It fell from the sky
> **2** Hot dish
> **3** The homesick cat
> **4** Eagle eyes

Follow up

● Dictate one or both of the explanations below to the class. Students then work in pairs or groups of three and discuss a situation for the explanation. They then write the beginning of the story. Discuss students' situations with the class. Then read out the situations below so that students can compare them with their own.

> **Explanations**
> **1** The couple were surprised and delighted! They had a very pleasant evening and enjoyed the concert very much. But when they returned home, they discovered that their house had been burgled and a lot of their possessions had been stolen.
> **2** As he was leaving, the old woman asked him, 'Before you go, could you help me find my pet hamster?' The young man went red. He said he was late for another appointment and rushed out of the door.
>
> **Situations**
> **1** A couple discovered that their car had been stolen. Next day, however, the car was back in front of their house. On the driver's seat there was a note. The writer of the note apologised for taking the car. He had had to take his mother to hospital. With the note were two tickets to a concert that night.
> **2** A young man was laying a fitted carpet in an old woman's living room. When he'd finished, he noticed a large lump in the middle of the carpet. The man didn't want to start again, so he took his hammer and attempted to flatten the lump. After a few hits with the hammer, the carpet was perfectly flat.

Situations

1 A couple came home one evening and discovered an enormous hole in their roof, their dog dead and their furniture covered in litres of horrible-smelling matter. Upset by what they saw, the couple phoned the police who soon arrived to investigate. After several phone calls, the detective was finally able to explain to the couple what had happened.

2 A man in San Diego bought a satellite dish and decided to set it up himself. He climbed up the ladder and attached the dish to the side of his house. Then, with his wife inside the house shouting to him when the reception was best, he adjusted it. When they were satisfied, the man and his wife relaxed for the evening in front of the TV. Even though the next day was very hot, the couple decided to stay at home and watch television. That afternoon they heard fire-engine sirens and lots of shouting outside. When they went outside, they saw that the house opposite was on fire. The fire was put out, but the firemen couldn't work out how the fire had started.

3 An old man from Hanover, Germany, had had enough of his cat. He was fed up with her scratching all the furniture and making a mess. So he gave her to a friend, who lived on the other side of town. He told his friend that he was getting too old to look after her. A week later, on a very cold winter day, the old man returned home from shopping and was surprised to see the cat shivering on his doorstep. The man was moved by the fact that his pet had found her way back from the other side of town in such cold weather. He took the cat inside and gave her lots of loving attention.

4 In Vancouver, Canada, a burglar broke into a house and had filled his bag with the owners' possessions when he suddenly felt a pair of eyes on him. Looking up, he saw an eagle staring at him with cold, merciless eyes. At first the man was too frightened to move, but after ten minutes he tried creeping towards the door. However, the eyes just followed him and he couldn't move.

Explanations

It seemed that the container holding the waste from the lavatories on a passing plane had burst open. The contents froze in the atmosphere as they fell towards the ground, and the resulting block of ice had smashed through the roof of the unlucky couple's house, killing their dog before melting all over their belongings.

The next day, however, a fire inspector was examining the burnt remains when a sudden flash of sunlight caught his attention. The inspector eventually worked out that the neighbour's satellite dish had been concentrating the sun's rays on the curtains of the house and had caused the fire. The man was fined $2,000 and forced to take down his satellite dish. The next year he got cable.

The next day, however, the old man met another friend, who asked him if he had found his cat. The old man said he had found her on his doorstep. His friend told him, 'Oh, well, I was on the other side of town when I saw your cat in the road. Although she hissed and struggled all the way, I drove her home and left her outside your door.'

Eventually, the homeowners returned and found the thief in their lounge. When the husband turned on the light, the thief could see that the eagle was stuffed. But it was too late and he was arrested. The homeowner commented, 'That dead eagle was better than any watchdog, I can tell you.'

4.3

Hi-tech homes

LEVEL
Upper-intermediate

TOPIC
Homes of the future

ACTIVITY TYPE
Students make
predictions and
check them in a text

**READING
FOCUS**
Reading for specific
information

TIME
40–50 minutes

KEY LANGUAGE
*computer geek, geek,
thumbs down,
thumbs up*

will future, active and
passive

PREPARATION
One photocopy for
each student – cut into
two parts (the Predictions
and the article)

Warm up

1 Explain to students that they are going to read about and discuss homes of the future.

2 Divide the class into pairs or groups of three. Students discuss homes of the future and make notes about their features.

3 Discuss predictions with the class. Students take turns to tell the class one prediction each. The other students say if they agree or disagree with the prediction.

Main activity

1 Give each student the list of Predictions. Students continue working in pairs or groups of three and check that their predictions are in the list. Tell them to add any of their predictions to the list if they are missing.

2 Elicit the meaning of *thumbs up* and *thumbs down*. Use gestures if necessary to make clear the meaning.

> **Answer key**
> *thumbs up*: yes   *thumbs down*: no

3 Explain that students are now going to read about a hi-tech home which actually exists. Read out the heading of the article *Geekhouse*. Explain that the dictionary definition of *geek* is a person who is boring and not fashionable, but the term *computer geek* is often used to describe someone who is obsessed with computers.

4 Read out the bi-line *Not every gadget in hi-tech home is a success*. Encourage students to suggest which features of a hi-tech home might not be a success.

5 Give each student the article. Students read the text and decide which of the predictions in the list are mentioned. They then decide which of the features got *thumbs up* and which got *thumbs down* in the original house. Encourage students to continue working together in pairs or small groups so that they can help each other.

6 Tell students to add to the list any features that are mentioned in the text, but are not already included in the list.

7 Discuss the answers with the class. Ask students if they are surprised by any of the changes that will be in the modified house.

> **Answer key**
> **List 2** down   **4** down   **5** down   **9** up
> **Text** always-on broadband Internet connection (Smart Board, webpads): up
> instant access to music, computer games, DVDs + central server: up
> automated doors: down
> remote-controlled washing machines: down
> Internet fridges: down
> face recognition door entry system: down
> remotely operated digital bath: down

Follow up

● Students rephrase the predictions given in the active voice in the passive, and vice versa. For example, *Gutters will collect rain water for washing and for drinking, Weather forecasts will be received by a satellite and passed on to the central heating unit.*

● Ask students if they would prefer to live in the original or the modified house.

Predictions

		In text	Up / Down
1	Rain water for washing and (after purification) for drinking will be collected in gutters.	...	...
2	A satellite will receive weather forecasts and pass them on to the central heating control unit.	...	...
3	The kitchen computer will store recipes, monitor food stocks and program the oven automatically.	...	...
4	Light switches will be activated by voice.	...	...
5	The toilet will analyse your output and give a health report.	...	...
6	An enclosed, temperature-controlled garden will protect plants from pollution.	...	...
7	A basement storage system will be run by a computer.	...	...
8	Dirt will be sucked into cleaning-system pipes in the walls and then collected in a central unit.	...	...
9	Homes will have an entertainment room with a wall-sized screen for viewing virtual-reality holograms.	...	...
10	There will be a soundproof module for teenagers.	...	...
11	Many people will work at home, so they will add office modules to their houses.	...	...
12	Automatic security shutters linked to sensors outside will be fitted to all windows.	...	...
13	....	...	...
14	....	...	...
15	....	...	...
16	....	...	...
17	....	...	...
18	....	...	...
19	....	...	...
20	....	...	...

Geekhouse

Not every gadget in hi-tech home is a success reports **Marc Ambasna-Jones**

In the middle of a Hatfield business park is Orange's hi-tech living laboratory where for the past 12 months, families have been watched Big Brother style, while they played with the latest gismos and gadgets. Four families have each spent no more than two weeks in the house. And based on their feedback, changes have been made to the house and less commercially viable technologies kicked out. The modified house will be a more realistic view of how families could live.

The families were filmed through wall-mounted cameras, and their behaviour and their use of technology was studied and analysed by academics from the Digital World Research Centre at Surrey University.

According to project manager, Jon Carter, by far the biggest success was the always-on broadband Internet connection and the ability to wirelessly access music, computer games and DVDs from a variety of rooms, controlled by a central server at the back of the house. In Mum and Dad's room, a large pull-down screen enabled DVD viewing or network gaming from the bed. An interactive Smart Board gave the daughter access to web games and control of her Sony Aibo dog. Mobile webpads were used as remote control and Internet access devices, and the large flat screen TV with access to TiVo's Digital Video recorder was "a big hit with all ages".

But not everything got such a positive report. While the company gained useful information on what people liked and wanted to use, it also discovered what people didn't want, and that's a bigger list. First of all, traditional light switches will replace the voice-activated ones of the original house. The same goes for a number of other home control areas. Automated doors will be replaced, especially after one family's dog got locked in the bathroom. Automated heating systems, remote-controlled washing machines and Internet fridges also got the thumbs down. The smart toilet that calls for an ambulance when it detects something sinister in the bowl got the thumbs down too. Carter also said that devices such as the face recognition door entry system and the remotely operated digital bath are "a long way off" in the minds of consumers.

In fact, Orange's once fully wired-up version of the future has been down-graded. The company's initial wish when it first built the house last year was to wire up everything. The four families that lived in the house have proved that people simply aren't ready for the kind of remote-controlled, automated world that was the original house. One thing is certain: our vision is now a little more realistic and it has ordinary people and not men in white coats to thank for that.

5.1

What does the sign say?

LEVEL
Elementary

TOPIC
Signs in town and country

ACTIVITY TYPE
Understanding signs

READING FOCUS
Understanding main message, identifying function, paraphrasing

TIME
40–50 minutes

KEY LANGUAGE
Imperatives

PREPARATION
One photocopy for each student; photos of typical town and country scenes; dictionaries

Warm up

1   Show the class photos of various typical town and country scenes. Ask students to say exactly where the photos were taken. Try to elicit the place names in Exercise A.

2   Show each photo to the class again. This time tell students to imagine that there is a sign in the photo. What could the sign say? Elicit suggestions, e.g. *No fishing* near a river.

3   Explain to students that they are going to look at some signs which can be found outdoors – either in a town or in the country.

Main activity

1   Give each student a photocopy. Ask students to match signs 1–12 with the places in Exercise A. Encourage students to use a dictionary where necessary and to work in pairs.

> **Answer key**
> **a)** 2   **b)** 6   **c)** 9   **d)** 8   **e)** 12   **f)** 7   **g)** 5   **h)** 4   **i)** 11   **j)** 10   **k)** 3   **l)** 1

2   Ask students to look at signs 13–18 and decide where they would find these signs. Point out that the six places are in the list in Exercise A.

> **Answer key**
> **13** in a street   **15** near a river   **17** on a beach
> **14** outside a farm   **16** at a railway station   **18** outside a building

3   Ask students to decide which sentence in Exercise B explains the main message for signs 13–18.

> **Answer key**
> **13** A   **14** B   **15** A   **16** A   **17** B   **18** B

4   Discuss different kinds of signs with the class. Write the headings from the chart below on the board. Use the notes and examples in the chart to explain the meaning of the headings.

information	prohibition	warning	instruction
tell you what something is for	tell you not to do something	tell you about danger	tell you to do something
EXIT	NO DIVING FROM BRIDGE	BEWARE OF THE BULL	PUT YOUR RUBBISH IN THE BIN

5   Ask students to put signs 13–18 into the four categories in the chart. Point out that some of the signs are in more than one category.

> **Answer key**
> **13** instruction / warning   **15** warning / prohibition   **17** instruction
> **14** information   **16** information / instruction   **18** information / instruction

6   Students put signs 1–12 into the four categories. They then write a sentence for each sign explaining the main message.

> **Answer key**
>   **1** prohibition – You must not cross here. You must use the subway.
>   **2** prohibition – You must not swim when the red flag is flying.
>   **3** information / instruction – Only private fishing here. Stay away from the water.
>   **4** warning – You must be careful. Rocks might fall.
>   **5** information – You can park here for 20 minutes if visiting the station.
>   **6** prohibition – You must not lean your bike against the window.
>   **7** warning / instruction – You must be careful. You must take care with cigarettes.
>   **8** information – You can buy strawberries, raspberries, potatoes and hay here.
>   **9** information – You can camp here for £10.00 or £15.00 per night.
>   **10** prohibition / information – You must not ride a horse or bike. You can only walk.
>   **11** information – You can enter the park between these hours.
>   **12** instruction – You must close the gate. You must keep your dog on a lead.

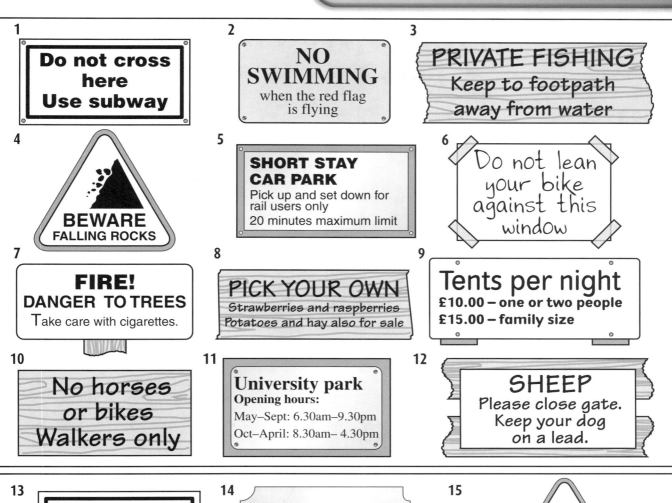

1 Do not cross here Use subway

2 NO SWIMMING when the red flag is flying

3 PRIVATE FISHING Keep to footpath away from water

4 BEWARE FALLING ROCKS

5 SHORT STAY CAR PARK Pick up and set down for rail users only 20 minutes maximum limit

6 Do not lean your bike against this window

7 FIRE! DANGER TO TREES Take care with cigarettes.

8 PICK YOUR OWN Strawberries and raspberries Potatoes and hay also for sale

9 Tents per night £10.00 – one or two people £15.00 – family size

10 No horses or bikes Walkers only

11 University park Opening hours: May–Sept: 6.30am–9.30pm Oct–April: 8.30am– 4.30pm

12 SHEEP Please close gate. Keep your dog on a lead.

13 Slow down! Children crossing

14 Orchard House Superior farmhouse accommodation

15 DANGER Shallow water No diving

16 ENTRANCE TO ALL PLATFORMS

17 Queue here for boats to Seal Island and Kittiwake Cove

18 Staff entrance VISITORS Please use door at front of museum

Exercise A

Look at signs 1–12. Match them with the places below.

a) on a beach
b) outside a building
c) at a campsite
d) outside a farm
e) by a field
f) in a forest
g) at a railway station
h) up a mountain
i) outside a park
j) near a path
k) near a river
l) in a street

Exercise B

Look at signs 13–18. Which sentence explains the message for each sign?

13 A You must drive slowly.
  B Children must walk slowly.

14 A You must stay here.
  B You can stay here.

15 A You must be careful in the water.
  B You must not go into the water.

16 A You must go through here to catch your train.
  B You must not go through here to catch your train.

17 A You cannot go to Seal Island.
  B You must wait here for a boat.

18 A Visitors can use this door.
  B Visitors must not use this door.

5.2

Where would you prefer to live?

LEVEL
Intermediate

TOPIC
City or country living

ACTIVITY TYPE
Note-taking

READING FOCUS
Speed-reading, recognising main ideas

TIME
30–40 minutes

KEY LANGUAGE
Past, present and future tenses

PREPARATION
One photocopy for each student; map of Britain

Warm up

1 Ask students if they are happy living where they do. Or would they prefer to live in a different environment? Explain to students that they are going to read about and discuss living in the city and living in the country.

2 Ask students *What are the good and bad points of living in a city?* Then ask *What are the good and bad points of living in the country?* Make four lists on the board.

3 Explain to students that they are going to read about the experiences of four people. Ask students to predict the kind of things the people will say. Use the headings in the chart in Answer key below (after 6) to guide them. Add the headings to a chart on the board as you discuss what the people will say. Then write the four names down the side of the chart.

Main activity

1 Give each student a photocopy. Allow students two minutes to find the names of four cities and four country areas in the text.

2 Check the answers with the class. Use a map of Britain to explain where the places are.

3 Tell students to copy the chart on the board. They then read the texts quickly to find the answers to the questions *Where does the speaker live now?* and *Where does the speaker want to live?* They complete the chart with either *city* or *country*.

4 Check the answers with the class and write them in the chart on the board. Make sure that students understand that Patrick was only on holiday in the Cotswolds.

5 Ask students to read the text again and make notes in the last column of the chart to show the reasons each speaker gives for wanting to live in the city or country. Remind students to use the four lists on the board that they discussed in the Warm up.

6 Check the answers with the class and write them on the board.

Answer key

	Where does the speaker live now?	Where does the speaker want to live?	What reasons does the speaker give for wanting to live in one environment and not the other?
Patrick	city	city	country = terribly quiet; very few people, nearest restaurant, cinema and theatre, 20-minute drive away
Alice	city	country	city = dirty and noisy country = fresh air and the views are out of this world
Nicola	country	country	country = everything she needs; no pub or restaurant near, but there are supermarkets in the nearest town city = had to wear a suit and tights every day; lived in a block of flats
Jake	country	city	country = nothing to do; nobody to do things with; only early buses to and from Nottingham city = will be able to go out with friends in the evening; won't have to get up so early

7 Ask students a) *Who talked about where they used to live?* b) *Who liked it?*

Answer key
a) Patrick, Nicola   b) Patrick

Follow up

● Tell students to imagine that a year has passed. Alice and Jake have both moved. But something has gone wrong, and life has not quite worked out as they imagined! Ask students to write a paragraph about where one of them lives now.

Where would you prefer to live? Write and tell us about your experiences.

Patrick: The best thing about travelling by train ... is that you get back to London at the end of it! I've just been to the Cotswolds for a week, and I couldn't get back to the city fast enough. The village where I was staying was terribly quiet. There were no shops, no restaurants and, it seems, hardly any people. Perhaps the houses were all holiday homes, and the owners were having a bad season. I don't know – I never found anyone to ask. I don't want to cook every evening when I'm on holiday – but the nearest restaurant was a 20-minute drive. That's not too far, you might say, but I'd gone by train. Perhaps there was a cinema and a theatre next to the restaurant – I never found those either. I've always lived in cities – the country is not the place for me.

Alice: I work as an architect. I went to university in Exeter and then just stayed on afterwards. I've been here for ten years now, but I don't really like the noise and dirt of city life. So, I'm selling my flat and moving to the Lake District. When I was a child, I used to visit my grandparents in the Lake District and I loved it. My grandfather and I went walking every day, and my grandmother taught me to swim in one of the lakes. My goodness, the water was cold! Three years ago, I met two other architects – at my grandfather's funeral, in fact. We got talking and soon became friends. I started visiting them at weekends, then they suggested that I move up there and start working with them. What an opportunity! The air is so fresh, and the views are out of this world. I can't wait to sell my flat.

Nicola: I'm an outdoor pursuits instructor and I share a cottage with three of my colleagues in Snowdonia. During the day, I teach canoeing, mountain-biking and rock-climbing. I love being outside. After work my friends and I take turns to cook a meal – we grow all our own vegetables – and then we play cards or watch TV. We've got everything we need here – it's true, there isn't a pub or restaurant for miles, but we're all reasonable cooks and there are supermarkets in the nearest town. I used to work in a solicitor's office, but I had to wear a suit and tights every day. I lived in a block of flats near the centre of Birmingham. I hated my old life. I don't know how I put up with it so long.

Jake: I'm eighteen years old and I live in a small village in the Peak District, not far from Nottingham. I live with my parents, and younger brother and sister. I grew up in this village, so I know everyone here. That's not the problem – the problem is that there's nothing to do, and nobody of my age to do it with! At the moment I travel into Nottingham every day to the shop where I work – there's a bus at 7.30 in the morning and the last bus back in the evening is at 5.30. From September, however, I'm going to stay in Nottingham with my aunt and uncle when my cousin goes into the Navy. I can use his room. I'm really looking forward to living in Nottingham – I'll be able to go out with my friends in the evening, and I won't have to get up so early in the morning.

5.3

LEVEL
Upper-intermediate

TOPIC
Wild animals that
have been found
in cities

ACTIVITY TYPE
Completing a text,
using clues to work
out the content of
another text

**READING
FOCUS**
Reading for detail,
information gap,
recreating a text

TIME
40–50 minutes

KEY LANGUAGE
*bushfire, freeway,
metropolitan area,
myth, suburban,
urban, wildlife*

PREPARATION
One photocopy for
each student – cut into
three parts (two
articles and the
wordcards, cut up into
a further sixteen
pieces)

Animal city dwellers

Warm up

1 Explain to students that they are going to read about and discuss animal city dwellers. Ask them to name any animals, domesticated or wild, that can be found in cities.

2 Also explain to students that they are going to work with a partner who has read a different article. They must not show their partner the article they have read.

Main activity

1 Divide the class into two halves, A and B. Give each student A: Big snapper takes bite of Big Apple and each student B: Koalas try suburban jungle. Tell students to read their text and guess the missing phrases. Encourage students to work together in pairs or small groups so that they can help each other.

2 Do not check the answers at this point. Instead give each student a set of wordcards. Explain that eight of these phrases go in the gaps in their text. Get them to match the eight phrases with the gaps. Again, do not check the answers at this point.

3 Divide the class into pairs so that each student A is working with a student B. Partners check that they have each chosen eight different phrases for the text-completion activity.

4 Check the answers with the class. The phrases on the worksheet are in the correct order.

5 Remind students that the other eight phrases go in the gaps in the article they haven't read. These provide useful clues as to its content.

6 Student A tells student B what they think article B is about. Then student B tells student A what they think article A is about. They can also ask questions to find out more information about the article they haven't read.

7 Students summarise orally the main points of the article they haven't read. They must use each of the eight phrases.

8 Give each student the article they haven't read.

Follow up

● Discuss the titles of the articles with the class. Elicit or explain that *Big Apple* is often used for New York. Explain that *jungle* can mean *an uncontrolled or confusing mass of things*. In the phrase *It's a jungle out there*, it means *Life is difficult and you have to fight for what you want*.

● Students continue working with their partner. They have to find three differences and three similarities between the articles. Give one or two examples to get them started, e.g. Difference: *Big snapper is about one animal while Koalas is about a group of animals*. Similarity: *Both texts mention an island*.

Big snapper takes bite of Big Apple

Michael Ellison
in New York

The nearest thing to confirming the urban myth that dangerous reptiles live below as well as above the pavements of New York emerged yesterday when a (1) .... alligator was discovered living in the wild.

Tom Lloyd, a contractor out for a stroll with his four-year-old daughter, saw a (2) .... that he took to be a toy among the ducks and geese in a stream on Staten Island. But when prodded with a stick, the object came alive and snapped at him.

The (3) .... of the creature – *alligator mississipiensis* – is North Carolina, four states away. "Somebody probably dumped him in there," said Bill Holmstrom, supervisor of Bronx zoo's reptile department.

Two police officers, directed by the city's resident (4) .... , Robert Shapiro, lassoed the 16kg gator's jaws, pulled it from the stream and taped its mouth shut.

Then they put the alligator, whose age was put at between two and five years, on the back seat of a squad car and drove it to the Manhattan (5) .... run by Mr Shapiro.

"He was hissing, but he wasn't darting at us or anything," said Mr Shapiro who has hundreds of unwanted reptiles in the back of the shop and deals with about five (6) .... crocodilians – alligators, crocodiles and caymans – each year. These have been handed over by owners who have decided that they can no longer look after them.

It has long been an urban myth that (7) .... of Manhattan live crocodiles and alligators which have been flushed down the sewers by owners who no longer want them.

"Animals need to be basking in the sun," said Mr Shapiro before the new find was (8) .... to a registered alligator keeper in Pennsylvania.

Koalas try suburban jungle

Koalas are lured by Adelaide

Patrick Barkham
in Sydney

In search of the perfect suburban lifestyle as well as plenty of (9) .... , koalas are deserting woodlands for backyards, bathrooms and cars in Adelaide.

Local conservationists have rescued 105 koalas from the suburban jungle (10) .... , compared with just 20 sightings of the bear-like marsupial in the city six years ago.

Cleland Wildlife Park's operations manager, Gary Fitzpatrick, said Australia's furry grey icon, a protected species and a rare sight in the wild, had flourished in the Adelaide Hills area since its introduction (11) ....

"With high numbers of koalas, competition for territory is increasing and male koalas are moving towards urban areas," he told the Adelaide Advertiser. "There's also much (12) .... in the metropolitan area now, which is attracting them."

But life in the suburbs is not all snoozing in backyards after a night spent snacking on garden gum trees. Instead of contending with bushfires, dingoes, pythons and (13) .... , the suburban koala must keep a beady eye out for dogs, roads and railways.

"There was one koala found on the South Eastern freeway – they just seem to skip across there without any fear," Mr Fitzpatrick said. But he also reported another case of a koala discovered dead on a railway line with its (14) ....

The clearing of native woodland has removed more than 80% of the koala's natural habitat, but in some areas where they were introduced to help preserve the species they have swiftly reached plague proportions, (15) .... with their voracious appetite for eucalyptus leaves.

Hundreds of koalas were airlifted off Kangaroo island in southern Australia (16) .... to save rare trees, birds and wildlife in the national park.

1.35 metre
long dark object
closest natural habitat
reptile rescue expert
T-shirt shop
illegally-owned
beneath the streets
sent on its way
eucalyptus leaves
so far this year
early last century
more vegetation
monitor lizards
arms sliced off
destroying trees
in 1997

6.1

Look behind you

LEVEL
Elementary

TOPIC
Urban myth about a
terrifying driving
experience

ACTIVITY TYPE
Ordering a story and
suggesting its ending

**READING
FOCUS**
Text organisation

TIME
40–50 minutes

KEY LANGUAGE
*engine, horn, indicator,
lights, mirror, seatbelt,
tyres, windscreen;
accelerate, brake,
check, clean, fasten,
flash, look in, overtake,
sound, start, swerve,
use*

Past tenses

PREPARATION
One photocopy for each
pair of students – cut
into two parts (the story
cut into thirteen strips
with the final strip kept
separate and the
Exercise); a magazine
advertisement of a car

Warm up

1   Explain to students that they are going to read about and discuss a car journey.

2   Begin the lesson by asking students to name parts of the car. Use a picture of a car from a magazine as a prompt.

3   Give each pair of students the picture and the Exercise. Tell students to complete the gaps with the verbs. Point out that they can use some of the verbs more than once.

4   Check the answers with the class. Get students to mime the actions, and draw diagrams on the board to illustrate the meaning of *overtake* and *swerve*.

Answer key	
You can	**Your car can**
check / clean / use / look in your mirror.	accelerate.
clean / check your tyres.	brake.
flash / use your indicator.	overtake.
use / clean / flash your lights.	swerve.
use / sound your horn.	
use / fasten your seatbelt.	
clean your windscreen.	
check / start your engine.	

Main activity

1   Give each pair of students the jumbled story. Tell students to put the parts of the story in order. When pairs of students have done this, they can compare their order with other pairs.

2   Check the order with the class. Get individual students to read out a sentence each.

3   Explain to the class that the final part of the story is missing. Ask students, working in their pairs again, to work out how the man had saved the woman's life. Tell them to write the final part of the story.

4   Get students to read out their ending to the class. Discuss the suggestions with the class. Then either give each pair of students the final part of the story, or read it aloud yourself. Then ask students to suggest a title for the story.

5   Ask students if they think the story is true. It seems too unlikely to be true. Explain that it is probably an urban myth – a story that is heard and repeated until nobody knows if it is true or not.

Follow up

●   Ask students if they know any urban myths. Do they think such stories are true?

●   Here is another urban myth about a driving experience. Read the first sentence and get students to predict what happened next. Then read the second sentence and get students to make another prediction. Repeat this procedure until you reach the end of the story.

> **Uphill all the way!**
> A man was driving to a job interview, but he got very lost.
> He decided to phone the company he had the interview with, but found that he had left his mobile at home.
> So he stopped his car at a phone box and phoned from there.
> He was explaining his problem to the secretary when his car started moving down the hill towards him.
> The man realised that he hadn't used the handbrake because he was in such a hurry.
> To the man's horror, the car crashed into the telephone box and locked him inside.
> When the secretary heard the man's shouting, she put the telephone down.
> The man waved to people on the street, but they just waved back.
> In the end, the man used the phone to call the fire brigade!

Exercise

accelerate   brake   check

clean   fasten   flash   look in   overtake

sound   start   swerve   use

You can		Your car can
.... your mirror.	.... your horn.	....
.... your tyres.	.... your seatbelt.	....
.... your indicator.	.... your windscreen.	....
.... your lights.	.... your engine.	....

Story Strips

A woman was driving home along a country road late one night.

The road was completely empty except for one car behind her.

The woman thought nothing of it until the other car began to overtake.

Then it suddenly braked, swerved back behind her and flashed its lights.

The woman felt a bit nervous, particularly when the car flashed its lights again.

She accelerated, but the other car stayed right behind her.

The woman was absolutely terrified by the time she got home.

And, what made things worse, the other car stopped behind her.

Her only hope of escaping was to get into the house and phone the police.

She got out of her car and began to run, but so did the driver of the other car.

She screamed in terror, but he shouted, 'Quick! Get inside and call the police!'

When the police arrived, the woman discovered that the man wasn't trying to kill her – he had actually saved her life.

As the man was driving along behind her, he had seen someone with a knife rising from the back seat. But when he flashed his lights, the person sat back down again.

6.2

Keeping in touch

LEVEL
Intermediate

TOPIC
A trip to New Zealand

ACTIVITY TYPE
Ordering e-mails and working out a traveller's itinerary

READING FOCUS
Extracting key information

TIME
40–50 minutes

KEY LANGUAGE
Past simple, *going to* and present continuous for the future; expressions of time

PREPARATION
One photocopy for each pair of students – cut into twelve parts (six e-mails and six photos); map of New Zealand

Warm up

1 Explain to students that they are going to read about and discuss a trip to New Zealand. They are going to read a set of e-mails and work out the writer's itinerary.

2 Ask if anyone has been to New Zealand. What did they do there? Ask other students what they know about New Zealand. Can they name any towns and cities? Explain that Auckland (on the North Island) is the largest city, but Christchurch (on the South Island) is the capital. Use the map, from the website mentioned in the Follow up, to show the location of these places.

Main activity

1 Divide the class into pairs. Give each pair of students a set of e-mails and a set of pictures. Explain that someone called Jane sent these e-mails to her friends back home in England. There was a photo of Jane attached to each e-mail. Students have to match the photos with the e-mails.

2 Check the answers with the class. The pictures on the worksheet are correctly matched with the e-mails. The e-mails are also in the correct order, but read out their openings, e.g. *We didn't go up in the helicopter yesterday*, in random order and get students to hold up the corresponding pictures.

3 Get students in their pairs to identify past events and future events in one of the e-mails. For example, *We didn't go up in the helicopter yesterday, it was too windy, we went for a walk on the glacier* are in the past, while *we're spending tonight and Sunday night, we're going to walk the Routeburn Track* are in the future.

4 Explain to students that they now have to put the e-mails into the correct order. Encourage them to identify the past and future events in each e-mail. Ask one student to read out the verb phrases which are about the past and the other to read out the verb phrases which are about the future.

5 While students are working, copy the dates in the chart below onto the board. Write *ARRIVAL* and *DEPARTURE* next to the first and last dates in the chart.

6 Check the order of the e-mails with the class. Then ask students to copy and complete the chart with the names of the places where Jane stayed.

7 Check the answers with the class. Use the map to confirm Jane's itinerary.

Answers			
Monday 1st	ARRIVAL Auckland	Thursday 11th	Queenstown
Tuesday 2nd	Auckland	Friday 12th	Routeburn
Wednesday 3rd	Rotorua	Saturday 13th	Routeburn
Thursday 4th	Rotorua	Sunday 14th	Queenstown
Friday 5th	Wellington	Monday 15th	Queenstown
Saturday 6th	Wellington	Tuesday 16th	Dunedin
Sunday 7th	Nelson	Wednesday 17th	Dunedin
Monday 8th	Nelson	Thursday 18th	Christchurch
Tuesday 9th	Franz Josef	Friday 19th	Christchurch
Wednesday 10th	Franz Josef	Saturday 20th	DEPARTURE

Follow up

- Students read the e-mails again and find the main activities of each day.

- Encourage students to find further information about New Zealand on the website: www.NZ.com. They can also research specific places. The website for the International Antarctic Centre is www.iceberg.co.nz, for example.

Greetings from New Zealand! We arrived in Auckland yesterday. This morning we went up Sky Tower. You can see the streets below because the floor is made of glass. Looking down gives you a very strange feeling. This afternoon we visited Mum's cousin. Tomorrow we're going to Rotorua. Will write again soon.

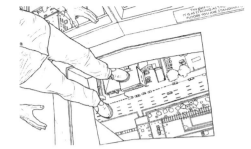

We arrived in Wellington an hour ago after an all-day journey from Rotorua. We spent two nights there. After arriving from Auckland the day before yesterday, we went to the hot springs – they're like a very smelly swimming pool! Yesterday we visited the Maori cultural centre and saw the geysers there. They throw hot water into the air every few minutes. Tomorrow we're going to Te Papa – the National Museum of New Zealand. I've heard that it's fantastic.

After two nights in Wellington we travelled to South Island by ferry. We took the coach to Nelson directly from the port and spent two nights with my boss's sister – she was very friendly. She took us to the Abel Tasman National Park yesterday. We spent the day on the beach. Very soon we're going to get on another coach – this time to Franz Josef. We're going to stay two nights there. We want to go up in a helicopter over the glaciers. It should be fun!

We didn't go up in the helicopter yesterday because it was too windy. Instead, we went for a walk on the glacier. We had to wear special boots because the ice was so slippery. We're now in Queenstown, where we're spending tonight and Sunday night. In between we're going to walk the Routeburn Track – this means staying two nights in huts. We have to carry our food, clothes and sleeping bag. I hope my rucksack isn't too heavy. We might stay two nights in Queenstown when we come back so that we can go tandem skydiving on Monday.

Skydiving was great! I'm glad we stayed an extra night in Queenstown. After all, it's not every day you jump 4,000 metres out of a plane! The Routeburn was OK, but we got very wet on our middle day. We travelled to Dunedin earlier today. Tomorrow we're going to the steepest street in the world. We're also going to take a boat trip to see some penguins and albatross – the biggest birds in the world. Then we're taking the coach to Christchurch the day after tomorrow. This holiday will soon be over!

We have spent two nights in Christchurch, and now we're at the airport. Yesterday we went to the cathedral, the museum and the park. We also bought our souvenirs – and another rucksack to carry them home! We checked in about three hours ago, then went to the International Antarctic Centre. This is a ten-minute walk from the terminal. I loved the ride on the Antarctic vehicle! See you very soon!

6.3

LEVEL
Upper-intermediate

TOPIC
Journeys with a difference

ACTIVITY TYPE
Separating and ordering stories

READING FOCUS
Speed-reading, text organisation, summarising, asking and answering questions about a text, recreating a text

TIME
40–50 minutes

KEY LANGUAGE
Past tenses

PREPARATION
One photocopy for each group of three students – cut into eighteen parts and jumbled

How stupid can you be?

Warm up

1 Explain to students that they are going to read and discuss three stories about journeys that went wrong. Ask them if they have made any journeys that went wrong. For example, have they ever got on a train going in the wrong direction?

Main activity

1 Explain to students that they are going to work in groups of three. Each person will read a different story. They must not show their story to the others in their group.

2 Give each group of three students the jumbled stories. Tell students that they have two minutes only to work out which six paragraphs belong to each story. Each student should collect the paragraphs for one of the stories.

3 Check the answers with the class. Read out the following lists of words, which show the first word of each paragraph in alphabetical order.

Answer key		
Story 1	**Story 2**	**Story 3**
but	a	and
even	as	at
he	anxiously	consequently
his	one	finally
on	thinking	in
the	when	soon

4 Ask students to work apart from their group and put the paragraphs of their story in order. Encourage students to work together in pairs or small groups with students who have the same story so that they can help each other. Tell students to write a 30-word summary of what went wrong in their story. Do not check the summaries at this point.

5 Students return to their original groups so that they are working again with the two students who have each read a different story.

6 Point out to students that after dividing the 18 paragraphs into three stories, they must know a little about the two stories that they haven't read. Explain that the two students who haven't read the story must ask their partner questions so that they can recreate the story. When they have done this, they then write a 30-word summary of what went wrong in each story.

7 Students continue working in their groups and compare their summaries. Are there any differences between the summaries?

> **Suggested summaries**
> 1 An Italian who had lived in San Francisco for years was travelling back to Italy. He got off the plane in New York and thought he was in Italy.
> 2 A businessman living in Tokyo thought his wallet had been stolen on the subway and attacked the pickpocket. His wife then told him he had left his wallet at home.
> 3 A man decided to fly on a lounge chair with helium balloons attached. Unfortunately, he dropped his air pistol so couldn't pop the balloons when he wanted to descend.

8 Give each student the stories they haven't read. Ask students if the stories have happy endings. And if so, who for?

> **Suggested answers**
> 1 Yes. Mr Scotti was taken back to Kennedy Airport, and we assume he reached Italy.
> 2 Happy for the businessman in that he got his wallet back, but not for the suspected pickpocket. He lost the lapels of his jacket.
> 3 Yes. He eventually began to descend, and landed right next to a swimming pool. This must mean, however, that he didn't reach his girlfriend's house.

Follow up

● Ask students to identify the point in each story where things went wrong. They then write an alternative, and much shorter, ending to the stories.

On the airplane was a very happy passenger. Mr Nicholas Scotti was going back to his native country of Italy after years of living in San Francisco.

A Western businessman living in Japan had been warned about pickpockets in the Tokyo subways. They grabbed wallets just as subway doors were closing, leaving the victim on the train, but without his money.

In early 1983, a man from the Los Angeles area had a great idea: Why not fly instead of drive to his girlfriend's house?

The plane made a refuelling stop at New York's Kennedy airport on its way to Italy. Mr Scotti, who didn't speak English too well, misunderstood the words 'refuelling stop'. Thinking he had arrived at his destination, he got off the plane and went into the airport.

One morning the Western businessman was at his usual subway stop when the train pulled in. He boarded, and sure enough, just as the train doors were about to close, he felt a man rub up against him.

And how would he do this? He would get a light pool lounge chair and attach helium balloons. Then he would simply float upward into the sky. He would take with him a beer – and an air pistol, to pop the balloons one by one when he wanted to lose altitude.

His nephews weren't there to meet him, but Mr Scotti assumed they had been caught in the notorious Roman traffic they had told him about in their letters. So he found his own way out of the airport.

Anxiously, the businessman reached for his wallet. It was gone! He looked up as the doors began to close and saw that the man who had rubbed against him had now stepped off the train.

At first, things went according to plan. The balloons rose, carrying the man and his lounge chair up into the sky. As the man achieved his desired altitude, he got ready to shoot a few balloons. He took aim … and then dropped the air pistol.

He *was* a little surprised at the changes there had been in Italy – but, after all, this was 1977 and it was natural to assume that many old buildings had been destroyed since he had left. He was also surprised by how many people spoke English, but, after all, American tourists were everywhere. There were even street signs in English!

Thinking fast, the businessman reached his hands between the closing train doors and grabbed the sneering thief's jacket lapels. The doors closed, with the thief still on the platform, but with his lapels trapped between the doors in the tight grip of the businessman.

Consequently, the lounge chair kept rising. At ten thousand feet, the winds took him out near the skies of LAX – Los Angeles Airport.

But Mr Scotti didn't have time for speculation. He had to meet his relatives. So he asked a police officer in Italian for directions to the bus terminal. The policeman, who by coincidence was from Naples, answered in fluent Italian. When he spoke to a second policeman, he wasn't so lucky. How ridiculous, thought Mr Scotti, that the government employed policemen who couldn't speak Italian.

As the train began to pull away, the pickpocket began screaming as he ran along the platform with the train. Finally, halfway along the platform, the thief grabbed the stanchion next to the door and his jacket lapels were torn off. As the train entered the tunnel, the businessman thought that at least he had got something for his loss.

Soon airline pilots began to report to the airport tower the unusual sight of a man in a lounge chair in the air lanes. One pilot reported a UFO – it was impossible that he could be seeing a man in a lounge chair with a beer at what was now fifteen thousand feet above the earth …

Even when Mr Scotti was told in Italian that he was in the wrong city and country, he wouldn't believe his mistake. As a police car rushed him back to the airport, he pointed at the speeding cars and said, 'I know I'm in Italy. That's how they drive.'

When he reached his office, he called his wife to get his credit card numbers so he could cancel them. 'You left your wallet on the table when you went to work today,' she told him.

Finally the winds blew the man and lounge chair back towards suburbia. And as the helium slowly leaked out of the balloons, the chair gradually began to descend, and then, fittingly, landed right next to a swimming pool.

7.1

Putting your eating habits to the test

LEVEL
Elementary

TOPIC
Healthy diets

ACTIVITY TYPE
Questionnaire completion

READING FOCUS
Making a personalised response

TIME
40–50 minutes

KEY LANGUAGE
alcoholic, baked, boiled, bread, butter, cheese, coffee, eggs, fish, fresh, fried, fruit, full-fat, grilled, juice, low-fat, meat, milk, pasta, roasted, skimmed, tea, vegetables, water, whole-meal

Present simple; expressions of quantity; adverbs of frequency; *should*

PREPARATION
One photocopy for each student – cut into two parts (the questionnaire and the key)

Warm up

1 Revise food and drink nouns. Ask each student to suggest a noun in turn. Make sure that they include the words in Key language.

2 Write these adjectives on the board: *alcoholic, fresh, full-fat, low-fat, skimmed, whole-meal.* Get students to match the adjectives with the food and drink items they have already mentioned. Then get them to say which food items can be *baked, boiled, fried, grilled, roasted.*

3 Practise expressions of quantity. Read out each expression on the left below. Get students to suggest another way of saying this (on the right).

Four or fewer   *Fewer than four*
Four or more   *More than four*
Between two and four *Two to four*

4 Read out these adverbs of frequency: *always, never, often, rarely, sometimes, usually.* Ask students to rank the adverbs in order from least frequent to most frequent.

> **Answer key**
> never, rarely, sometimes, often, usually, always

5 Ask students to predict what they are going to read about and discuss in the lesson. Explain that they are going to answer a questionnaire about their diet and find out how healthy they are. Encourage students to say whether they are healthy eaters or not.

Main activity

1 Give each student the questionnaire. Allow students time to read the questions. Look at question 6 with the class. Make sure that students understand that a *serving* is a portion, e.g. *an apple, a glass of orange juice, a plate of salad, some carrots with their meal,* etc.

2 Divide the class into pairs. Partners take turns to ask and answer the questions. They note their partner's answers.

3 When students have completed the questionnaire and worked out how many answers of each letter their partner has, give them the key. Partners look at the key together and work out how good their diets are.

4 Discuss the results with the class. Is anyone surprised by the results?

Follow up

● Read out each of the following pieces of advice. Ask students if they need to follow this advice. Point out that anyone who has answered A or B to questions 1–4 will need to follow this advice.

> **Advice**
> **1** You should drink more glasses of water.
> **2** You should drink fewer cups of tea and coffee.
> **3** You should eat fresh whole-meal bread or pasta more often.
> **4** You should eat fried food less often.

Students then write similar advice for the remaining questions where their partner answered A or B.

Putting your eating habits to the test

Do you pay enough attention to your diet? Answer the following questions to find out whether you are giving your body what it needs or putting your health at risk.

1 How many glasses of water do you drink every day?

- A Three or fewer
- B Four to seven
- C Eight or more

2 How many cups of coffee and tea do you drink every day?

- A Eight or more
- B Between four and seven
- C Fewer than four

3 How often do you eat whole-meal bread or pasta?

- A Rarely or never
- B Often or sometimes
- C Usually or always

4 How often do you eat fried foods instead of grilled, boiled, baked or roasted?

- A Usually or always
- B Often or sometimes
- C Rarely or never

5 On average, how many alcoholic drinks do you have every day?

- A More than four
- B Two or three
- C One or none

6 How many servings of fruit and vegetables do you have every day, including juice?

- A Fewer than two
- B Two, three or four
- C Five or more

7 How often do you eat fast food instead of healthier meals?

- A Usually or always
- B Often or sometimes
- C Rarely or never

8 How often do you eat fresh fish?

- A Rarely or never
- B Once every month or two
- C More than once a week

9 How many eggs do you eat every week?

- A Four or more
- B Two or three
- C Fewer than two

10 How many servings of dairy produce – butter, milk, cheese, and red meat – do you have every day?

- A More than eight
- B Three to seven
- C Two or fewer

11 How many sugary foods and drinks do you have every day, including sugar in tea and coffee?

- A More than eight
- B Between three and seven
- C Fewer than two

12 How often do you choose low-fat over full-fat alternatives, such as skimmed milk for full-fat milk?

- A Rarely or never
- B Three to seven
- C Whenever possible

Putting your eating habits to the test: the key

Count up how many As, Bs and Cs you have at the end. Read the corresponding advice to find out how your eating habits rate and what you can do to improve them.

Mostly As

You need to pay more attention to your diet – consuming too much fat, sugar and processed foods increases your risk of illness and can lead to weight problems and a loss of health and energy. If you want to live a longer and healthier life, change your eating habits.

Mostly Bs

Although you are watching your diet and are probably aware of the health risks involved in eating certain foods, you need to make a greater effort to eat well most of the time. Look at the questions to which you answered A or B. Note the things you need to change.

Mostly Cs

Well done! You clearly think about what you eat and are aware of how it affects your body functioning and health. If you answered A or B to any of the questions, however, you should take steps to improve these aspects of your diet.

7.2

LEVEL
Intermediate

TOPIC
Food-and-drink
quotations

ACTIVITY TYPE
Matching beginnings
and endings of
quotations

**READING
FOCUS**
Sentence structure,
paraphrasing

TIME
30–40 minutes

KEY LANGUAGE
balanced diet,
packaging materials,
table manners,
teetotaller

PREPARATION
One photocopy for
each pair of students –
cut into two parts (the
Quotation beginnings
and the Quotation
endings, with the
endings cut into twelve
strips)

It's not what you eat and drink … it's what you say

Warm up

1 Write the following words from the worksheet on the board: *table manners, packaging materials, teetotaller, balanced diet*. Elicit or explain the meaning of the words. Ask students to predict what the lesson is about (food and drink).

Main activity

1 Explain to students that they are going to read and discuss some quotations about food and drink. Point out that such quotations are often noted for their general truth, and/or humour!

2 Give each pair of students the list of Quotation beginings.

3 Use the Notes below to provide background information about the sources. Explain that *Anon.* is an abbreviation for *Anonymous* and is used when the writer's name is not known.

4 Encourage students to predict what word or what kind of word may come next. In quotation 1, for example, the next word is most likely to be an adjective, an article (*a/an, the*) or a pronoun (*what, when*).

5 Students work in their pairs and predict the endings of the quotations. They write their endings in a list.

6 Give each pair of students the set of Quotation endings. Tell students to match the endings with the beginnings.

7 Check the answers with the class. Get individual students to read out a full quotation each.

8 Ask students to paraphrase the quotations.

Suggested answers
1 If you're hungry, you really enjoy your food.
2 I don't like ordinary things; I like special things.
3 In England, they don't have good food.
4 Eating well has a positive effect on our lives.
5 Don't make children eat food they don't like.
6 People eat mainly packaged food.
7 Everyone likes chocolate.
8 Poor diets can kill us.
9 You don't know how your life will develop.
10 Play on words – 'weigh' and 'way'.
11 Play on the word 'balanced'.
12 Enjoy your food while you can.

Follow up

● Discuss the quotations with the class. Which do students particularly like? Which do they agree with? Are any of their own endings better than the originals?

Notes
1 Cervantes (1547–1616) Spanish novelist [*Don Quixote* (1605) part 2, chapter 5]
2 George Bernard Shaw (1856–1950) Irish playwright [*Candida* (1898) act 3]
3 George Mikes (1912–) Hungarian-born writer [*How to be an alien* (1946) page 10]
4 Virginia Woolf (1882–1941) English novelist [*A room of one's own* (1929)]
5 Katherine Whitehorn (1928–) English journalist
6 *The Economist* weekly economic-and-political journal
7 John G. Tulliss (1953–) American artist and cartoonist
8 Samuel Smiles (1812– 86) English writer [*Duty* (1880) chapter 16]
9 *Forrest Gump* (1994) film starring Tom Hanks as American simpleton

Quotation endings

Quotation beginnings

1 Hunger is
Cervantes

the best sauce in the world.

2 I'm only a beer teetotaller,
George Bernard Shaw

not a champagne teetotaller.

3 On the Continent people have good food;
George Mikes

in England they have good table manners.

4 One cannot think well, love well, sleep well
Virginia Woolf

unless one has dined well.

5 A food is not necessarily essential
Katherine Whitehorn

just because your child hates it.

6 With packaging materials in short supply,
The Economist

people may have to eat fresh food.

7 Nine out of ten people like chocolate.
John G. Tulliss

The tenth person always lies.

8 We each day
Samuel Smiles

dig our graves with our teeth.

9 My mama said life was like a box of chocolates.
Forrest Gump

You never knew what you'd get.

10 A diet is
Anon.

a weigh of life.

11 A balanced diet is
Anon.

a cookie in each hand.

12 Eat, drink and be merry for
Anon.

tomorrow you diet.

7.3

LEVEL
Upper-intermediate

TOPIC
Humorous approach
to dieting

ACTIVITY TYPE
Prediction and text
completion

**READING
FOCUS**
Text structure
and coherence,
identifying humorous
ideas

TIME
40–50 minutes

KEY LANGUAGE
*calorie consumption,
crash diet, diet,
junk food,
visualisation technique*

PREPARATION
One photocopy for
each pair of students –
cut into three parts
(the text, the Sentence
beginnings and the
Sentence endings)

How to diet

Warm up

1 Explain to students that they are going to read about and discuss dieting. Ask if any of them have been on a diet. *What was their diet? What was it like? Did it work? Can they give any advice to anyone else who is thinking of going on a diet?*

2 Give each pair of students the Sentence beginnings. Go through an example with the class. Discuss the first sentence and get individual students to suggest ways of completing the sentence. Students then work with their partner and complete the other sentences in their own words.

3 Compare some, but not necessarily all, of students' suggested sentence endings.

Main activity

1 Give each pair of students the text. Explain that students have to check whether their sentence endings fit into the text. They can modify any of their endings if they no longer make sense within the text.

2 Give each pair of students the Sentence endings. Explain that students have to match the sentence endings with the gaps in the text. Go through an example with the class. Ask students to find the missing ending for gap 3. (See Answer key below.)

3 Ask students to complete the text with the sentence endings.

4 Check the answers with the class.

> **Answer key**
> **1** d) **2** f) **3** k) **4** l) **5** b) **6** e) **7** h) **8** c) **9** i) **10** g) **11** a) **12** j)

5 Ask students to identify the writer's function in creating this text. The main function is to amuse, rather than to inform. Then ask them to identify which parts of the text they find amusing and to explain why.

> **Suggested answers**
> **1** Dieters are going round in circles here!
> **2** The writer must have been on trains where there is no food.
> **4** People use hundreds of excuses for eating biscuits.
> **5** Can you think of anything to eat which includes the letter X? The answer is no!
> **7** Not by much!
> **9** If your jaws are wired together, you'll sound funny.
> **10** Nobody is suggesting that we should chew things 380 times. Taking a week to eat a cheese sandwich is ridiculous.
> **11** You don't store food elsewhere. Your stomach expands to hold the food that you eat.
> **12** A chocolate bar is much bigger than a stick of celery. You'd expect to get a small reward if you have done something good.

Follow up

● Students continue working in pairs and invent an excuse for eating biscuits. Give an example yourself, e.g. *I had to eat this biscuit. It was lonely in the packet on its own.* Encourage students to make their excuses as amusing as possible. They then take it in turns to tell the class their excuse(s). Students vote for the funniest excuse(s).

How to diet

The purpose of dieting is to lose weight, so that you (1) .... Lots of people overeat because (2) .... A good way to reduce your calorie consumption is (3) .... A train, for example.

There are more different diets (4) .... There's the F-Plan, C-Plan, etc. The most effective diet is (5) .... One useful tip is to (6) .... This is really good for big eaters because (7) .... .Finally, when you've finished the list, eat it. That's your meal for the day. Crash diets are where you can lose a stone in a week. This is otherwise known as amputation.

For the really serious you can (8) .... But remember that doing this (9) ....

You'll eat less if you learn to chew slowly and savour your food. You will cut down your food intake drastically if (10) .... Avoid using this technique during important business lunches.

I'm following a new revolutionary diet!

A great idea to make you think twice about eating is to consider (11) .... For example, imagine that huge slice of chocolate cake being stored on your thighs. Go easy with this visualisation technique because you might start to associate your thigh with chocolate cake and wake up to find yourself munching away at your leg.

You can also try a treats system where (12) .... Really fat people who eat nothing but junk food are using the same system: they reward themselves with tasty junk food all their lives and punish themselves by an early death.

Sentence beginnings

1 The purpose of dieting is to lose weight, so that you …

2 Lots of people overeat because …

3 A good way to reduce your calorie consumption is …

4 There are more different diets …

5 The most effective diet is …

6 One useful tip is to …

7 This is really good for big eaters because …

8 For the really serious you can …

9 But remember that doing this …

10 You will cut down your food intake drastically if …

11 A great idea to make you think twice about eating is to consider …

12 You can also try a treats system where …

Sentence endings

a) where you're going to store the food you eat when your stomach is already full.

b) the X-Plan diet, however; you can eat anything as long as it has an X in it.

c) have your jaws wired together, which means you have to exist on energy drinks.

d) will become more attractive to the opposite sex, who will then invite you out to expensive restaurants where you can eat like a hog.

e) keep a list of everything you eat.

f) food is never more than a 30-second walk away, in our abundant society.

g) you chew each mouthful 380 times, as it will take you a week to get through a cheese sandwich.

h) compiling the list can cut down the time you spend eating.

i) might also have a detrimental impact and negative effect on your career in telesales.

j) you punish yourself with a stick of celery for lunch and reward yourself with a chocolate bar for afters.

k) to locate yourself in wilderness where there is no food.

l) nowadays than excuses to eat biscuits.

8.1

How do I look?

LEVEL
Elementary

TOPIC
Profile of a circus
performer

ACTIVITY TYPE
Reading
comprehension

**READING
FOCUS**
Skimming for gist,
recognising main
ideas, text cohesion

TIME
40–50 minutes

KEY LANGUAGE
caravan, circus, clown,
costume, host, monkey,
perform, performance,
performer, show, train,
trainer, training

Present simple; past
simple

PREPARATION
One photocopy for
each student

Warm up

1   Tell students that they are going to read a magazine article about someone who works in a circus. Write the word *circus* on the board. Get students to suggest words associated with *circus*, e.g. *clown, monkey,* and write them on the board. Introduce the words in Key language if students don't mention them themselves.

Main activity

1   Give each student a photocopy. Ask students a) *What is the name of the woman in the photo?* b) *What is her job?*

> **Answer key**
> **a)** Nell Gifford   **b)** circus performer

2   Look at the paragraph headings in A with the class. Students then read the text and match the headings with the paragraphs.

> **Answer key**
> **a** 5   **b** 4   **c** 1   **d** 3   **e** 2

3   Ask students to read the text again. They find the words in the text from B and work out what they refer to.

> **Answer key**
> **1** when I was a child   **4** the wagon
> **2** monkeys   **5** during the performances
> **3** Nell and her husband Toti   **6** sitting on my bed and doing nothing

4   Tell students to underline the sentences in the text about the past. Get individual students to read out a sentence each. Make sure that students understand *taught, bought* and *restored*. Encourage them to work out the meaning from context and to help each other if necessary.

5   Ask students to answer the questions in C.

> **Answer key**
> **1** when she was a child   **4** her husband Toti
> **2** a monkey trainer   **5** in a terrible state
> **3** at the Circus Roncalli in Germany   **6** restored it

6   Allow students time to read the text again and answer the questions in D.

> **Answer key**
> She is a horse-rider. She also trains horses, designs the costumes and is the show's host.

7   Ask students to answer the question in E. In order to encourage students to talk about Nell's clothes, make-up and state of mind, ask them *What does she wear? What about her face? How does she hope to feel?*

> **Answer key**
> She hopes to look glamorous in her costume. She hopes her make-up is perfect. She hopes to feel relaxed.

Follow up

●   Ask students if they would like to work in a circus. Why? / Why not?

How do I look?

Nell Gifford, circus performer

© Andrew Fox / The Independent

1 I get up early every morning and practise on my horse. Perlo is a very good horse. He kneels, stands on his back legs, goes backwards and sideways. I learned to ride when I was a child. But I didn't want to work with horses then. I wanted to be a monkey trainer. I had about 30 toy monkeys. The circus is now my life – but I don't want to work with monkeys. I understand that they are very difficult to train. I studied at the Circus Roncalli in Germany under Yasmin Smart. She taught me a lot about training circus horses.

2 My husband Toti and I started Giffords Circus in 1999. I design the costumes for the show. I use many different things – short skirts, fancy jackets, ballet shoes, feathers in our hair. We all look very glamorous. Dressing up for the show is wonderful.

3 As a circus performer, you have to wear a lot of make-up, too. I wear a lot on my eyes and I like it to be perfect. It's really important to clean your skin after wearing make-up. But sometimes I'm very tired at night, and I forget to remove it.

4 Toti and I live in a 1940s wooden wagon. The wagon was in a terrible state when we bought it. We restored it, and now it's like a little flat. It's small, but very warm, with a TV, cooker and electric heating. It's also got running water – much better than most circus caravans.

5 You have to be fit in a circus. The work is very hard, so you have to look after yourself. We do a two-hour afternoon and evening performance every day. I need to be at my best then. For half an hour before each show, I like sitting on my bed and doing nothing. I have to relax like this because I'm both a performer and the host!

A Read the text. Match the headings (a–e) with the paragraphs.

a My health   **b** My home   **c** My life with horses   **d** My face   **e** My clothes

B What do these words refer to?

1 then (para 1)   **2** they (para 1)   **3** we (para 4)   **4** it (para 4)   **5** then (para 5)   **6** this (para 5)

C Underline the sentences in the text about the past. Then answer these questions.

1 When did Nell learn to ride?
2 What did she want to be when she was a child?
3 Where did she learn to train circus horses?
4 Who did she start Giffords Circus with?
5 What was the wagon like when Toti and Nell bought it?
6 What did they do to the wagon?

D Nell is a circus performer. What kind of performer is she? What three other things does she do in her job?

E Nell asks: *How do I look?* How does she hope to look at the beginning of a show?

8.2

His or hers?

LEVEL
Intermediate

TOPIC
Escape from a
prisoner-of-war
camp

ACTIVITY TYPE
Ordering a story

**READING
FOCUS**
Text organisation

TIME
40–50 minutes

KEY LANGUAGE
*barbed wire, belt,
camp, canteen, cap,
Commandant, gate,
hat, jacket, leggings,
mackintosh, muff,
password,
prisoner of war, sentry,
skirt, soldiers, tunnel,
veil, waistcoat*

Past tenses

PREPARATION
One photocopy for
each pair of students –
cut into two parts (the
story and the Exercise
with the story cut into
ten strips)

Warm up

1   Revise items of clothing, including the items in Key language. Write these items on the board: *belt, cap, hat, jacket, leggings, mackintosh, muff, skirt, veil, waistcoat.* Ask students if these items are men's or women's clothing.

> **Answer key**
> *skirt, muff, veil* are women's; the rest are men's and women's

2   Write *barbed wire* on the board. Elicit or explain the meaning of *barbed wire*. Ask students where you find *barbed wire*. Elicit or explain the meaning of *camp*. Ask students to suggest a link between *barbed wire* and *camp*. Repeat this procedure with the other words: *canteen, Commandant, gate, password, prisoner of war, sentry, soldiers, tunnel.* Encourage students to predict the topic of the story they are going to read.

Main activity

1   Give each pair of students the Story strips. Tell students to put the paragraphs of the story in order.

2   Check the order with the class. Read out the first sentence or phrase from each paragraph in order.

3   Explain that the prisoner was called Heinz Justus and that this is a true story. Ask students to read the text again and to make a list of everything Heinz wore when he was disguised as a) Mr Budd, and b) the woman.

4   Check the answers with the class.

> **Answer key**
> **Mr Budd** leggings, cap, mackintosh, bag, spectacles
> **woman** hat, muff, veil, jacket, skirt, belt

5   Give each pair of students the Exercise. Ask students to discuss the questions in their pairs. Encourage them to answer the questions from memory, and then to return to the text to check what they remember and for further details. Explain that their answers should form a summary of the text.

6   Check the answers with the class. Get individual students to give one part of the summary each.

> **Answer key**
> 1 He decided to escape from the camp by disguising himself as the canteen manager, Mr Budd.
> 2 He decided to dress as a woman after his escape because men had to have a pass if they wanted to travel by train, and he wanted to go to London.
> 3 He began collecting the woman's disguise in the camp, and he made the clothes out of an old blanket and fur waistcoats.
> 4 On the day of his escape, he wore leggings, a mackintosh and a cap, and carried a bag. He also wore a false moustache and spectacles, and smoked a pipe like Mr Budd.
> 5 He decided to leave the camp at ten to eight because Mr Budd always left at eight.
> 6 Heinz's friends kept Mr Budd busy in the canteen until shortly after eight.
> 7 The sentry didn't ask Heinz for the password because he thought he was Mr Budd.
> 8 No. When Mr Budd left the camp a short time later, there would be a different sentry on duty because the sentries were usually changed at eight o'clock.
> 9 He decided to change into the woman's clothes before he got to Masham station.
> 10 When the soldiers spoke to him, they knew from his voice that he was the escaped prisoner.

Follow up

●   Ask students what they think of the story. What kind of man was Heinz? Would they have tried to escape like he did?

●   Ask students if they know of any other famous escape stories.

Story strips

I was taken as a prisoner of war in July 1917 to Colsterdale camp, near Masham, and I didn't want to stay there. I tried several times to get through the barbed wire and I also took part in one of the tunnelling schemes which was, however, discovered by the British just before the tunnel was completed.

Then one day I had an idea – I would walk out through the gate disguised as our English canteen manager, Mr Budd. So I started watching him as he left the camp every evening. I noticed that the sentries never asked him for the password. Everybody knew Mr Budd too well for that. This was also, of course, rather a drawback; but my idea was to escape in the evening after dark.

I understood that every male passenger in those war days had to produce a document when buying a railway ticket, particularly when travelling to London. As I didn't want to walk there, I decided to travel as a woman.

Then I heard that Mr Budd was going to be sent to another camp. I had no time to lose, so I began collecting an outfit in the camp. My skirt was made out of an old blanket, and the hat and muff were mostly composed of parts of fur waistcoats.

The day of the escape arrived and I put on all the clothes, man and woman's mixed together. I approached the gate disguised as Mr Budd. I wore a false moustache and a pair of spectacles in exactly the way Mr Budd wore them. My cap, mackintosh and bag were also exact replicas of the ones with which Mr Budd used to leave the camp every evening. My friends all thought I really was Mr Budd when they saw me.

Mr Budd used to leave the camp at about 8 pm, so I decided to leave at about ten minutes to eight. Some friends of mine would keep the real Mr Budd busy in the canteen until shortly after eight. As the sentries were usually changed at eight o'clock sharp, I was sure that the new sentry would not be surprised to see the second and real Mr Budd leaving the camp. So I walked to the gate smoking my pipe as if I were Mr Budd after a day's work at the canteen. I shouted 'Guard' as Mr Budd did. The sentry called out, 'Who's there?' 'Budd,' I answered. 'Right,' he said and opened the big door.

I walked slowly away from the camp. It was a two-hour walk to Masham station; but I had only gone a short distance when I saw our Commandant coming towards me. I tore off the moustache and spectacles as, of course, I didn't want the Commandant to address the false Mr Budd. As I passed him, I just said 'Good evening', and so did he.

A little further on I decided to change into a woman. I exchanged Mr Budd's cap with the woman's hat and veil which I carried in my bag, and took off my mackintosh, which covered a blue jacket, trimmed with all sorts of lace and bows. My skirt was held up with a leather belt round my hips, so I undid the belt and released the skirt. Luckily for me skirts in those days reached down to the ground, so my leggings were completely covered by the skirt and couldn't be seen in the dark.

After some time I noticed three soldiers following me. They were from the camp. I thought about throwing away my bag, but this was impossible. The soldiers came closer and closer until finally they overtook me. They then stopped and said 'Good evening, miss. Have you by any chance seen a man with a bag like yours? A prisoner of war has escaped and we are out looking for him.'

I tried for a time to speak in a high voice, asking them not to speak to a woman on her own. Could they have a look at the bag I carried? I refused, of course, but I knew that it was all over with me. I was found out.

Exercise

1 How did Heinz decide to escape from the camp?

2 Why did he decide to dress as a woman after his escape?

3 How did he get the woman's disguise?

4 On the day of his escape, how did he disguise himself as Mr Budd?

5 Why did he decide to leave at ten to eight?

6 How did Heinz's friends help him?

7 Why didn't the sentry ask him for the password?

8 Would the real Mr Budd go past the same sentry?

9 When did Heinz change into the woman's clothes?

10 What happened when the soldiers spoke to him?

8.3

LEVEL
Upper-intermediate

TOPIC
Cosmetic surgery

ACTIVITY TYPE
Note-taking

READING FOCUS
Reading for detail, identifying topic sentence

TIME
40–50 minutes

KEY LANGUAGE
None

PREPARATION
One photocopy for each group of four students – cut into eight parts

What do men really think of cosmetic surgery?

Warm up

1 Explain to students that they are going to read about and discuss cosmetic surgery. On which parts of the body do people have cosmetic surgery? What do students think of cosmetic surgery? Do they know anyone who has had it?

2 Explain that students are going to read the views of eight men. Ask students to predict what kind of things the men will say. Use the headings in the chart in Answer key below to guide students. Build up a chart on the board as you discuss what the men will say.

Main activity

1 Divide the class into groups of four. Give each group a set of opinions. Tell students to copy the chart on the board and complete it with information about each man. Point out that sometimes in response to the *Yes/No* questions, they may have to answer *information not given* or *not relevant*, or another answer other than *yes* or *no*. Encourage students to work together in pairs within the group so that they can help each other.

2 Check the answers with the class and complete the chart on the board.

Answer key

What's his name?	What's his partner's name?	Has she had surgery?	Does she want to?	On which part of the body?	Has he had surgery?	Is he in favour?
Darren	Nicola	no	yes	nose	no	no
Joel	Lyndsey	information not given	information not given	information not given	no	no
Steve	single	not relevant	not relevant	not relevant	no	no
Simon	Rebecca	yes	she's had it	face (wrinkles)	yes	not really
Richard	Sarah	no	information not given	information not given	no	no
Michael	Linda	yes	she's had it	face, neck, eyes	yes	yes
Andy	Sandra	no	yes	face	no	no
James	Alison	no	perhaps	information not given	no	yes

3 Explain to students that this article is from the British magazine *Woman*. In the article, each view was accompanied by a caption, i.e. a sentence or phrase from the article which summarised the writer's view. This was short and snappy, eight words at the most, sometimes it included the word *I*, but never referred to the writer's partner. Give one or two examples from Answer key in 5 below.

4 Ask students to continue working in their groups and get them to suggest the best caption for each view.

5 Discuss the answers with the class. The original captions from *Woman* are given below. If students' suggestions are different, this does not necessarily mean that they are wrong.

Answer key
Darren – Why go under the knife needlessly?
Joel – It looks so unnatural
Steve – Having a tummy tuck is lazy
Simon – I'm convinced I wouldn't notice
Richard – I hate the 'Hollywood' look
Michael – I'm a cosmetic surgery convert
Andy – People should grow old gracefully
James – I'd have surgery if I had the money

Darren Appleby, a 31-year-old art director, is married to Nicola, 30. They live in Cheshire.

Nicola loathes her nose and would love surgery to make it smaller, but even if I was the richest man in Britain I wouldn't pay for her to have it done. Aside from the fact that I love her exactly the way she is, why go under the knife needlessly? It seems so vain. Any operation is worrying, so I wouldn't want her to be put at risk unnecessarily. Nicola knows how I feel, so I'd be really upset if she had surgery behind my back – she'd no longer look like the woman I fell in love with.

Joel Orme is a 24-year-old television researcher. He lives in Manchester with his girlfriend Lyndsey Evans, 24.

Nine times out of ten, you can tell if a woman's had cosmetic surgery, particularly a facelift, because it looks so unnatural. But nose jobs are the worst – they usually look like they've been stuck on. As a child, I used to get teased because my ears stick out a bit. I asked my dad if I could have them pinned back and he always said no. I'm glad he did now, because I realise they're part of what makes me who I am.

Steve King, 28, lives in London and works in the media. He's single.

I don't have a problem with anyone having surgery to pin back their ears, but having a tummy tuck is lazy and could be sorted out with healthy eating and exercise. I also question the reasons some people have surgery. For example, if a woman is unhappy with her appearance and it's having a psychological effect on her, then there's nothing wrong with doing something about it. But surgery just to please a boyfriend is simply ridiculous.

Simon Wells, 44, and Rebecca Owen, 59, both teachers, live in London.

I hadn't really noticed Rebecca's wrinkles – it was the lines on my forehead that people usually commented on. But after she read about procedures to iron out lines, she suggested we both tried it. I was more impressed with the results than she was, but I won't have any more. I don't mind if Rebecca wants to, but only if she does it for herself. I'm convinced I wouldn't notice a new haircut, never mind a smoother face.

Richard Shorney, 40, a business adviser, lives in Cambridgeshire with his wife Sarah, 32.

Women always aspire to look like celebrities, but I bet most stars have spent a fortune making themselves that way. I hate the 'Hollywood' look – women with rigid faces from too many facelifts. They look like clones of each other. I actually think it's individuality and the imperfections that make women beautiful. I wouldn't want Sarah to have plastic surgery, even though there are bits of her she doesn't like. I think she's great the way she is.

Michael Briggs, 56, is married to Linda, 48. They run a website business together and live in Norfolk.

Linda had cosmetic surgery three years ago. I was dead against it and worried about the health aspect more than anything. She had a lower face and neck lift, an upper and lower eye lift, laser treatment to remove fine lines and excess fat removed from around her eyes. She was battered and bruised afterwards, but once everything settled down she looked amazing. Since then I've had cosmetic dentistry to realign my teeth and I'm about to have excess fat and skin removed from my upper eyelids. I'm a cosmetic surgery convert.

Andy Barden, 35, lives in Kent with his wife Sandra, 46.

Sandra's going to have a facelift later this year and nothing I say will change her mind. I don't think she needs it and I really can't understand why she wants to put herself at risk. There's also the fact it's so expensive and there are far better things to spend the money on. We've had a few arguments about it, but I'm resigned to the fact that she'll go ahead. I just don't think looks are that important – it's what a person is like on the inside that counts – people should grow old gracefully. Cosmetic surgery seems such a vain thing to do.

James Palmer, 32, is a farmer from Cambridge. He's married to Alison, 27.

There's no need to be unhappy with your appearance these days. I'd have surgery if I had the money. I'd have the bump on my nose removed, although I'd never have pectoral implants to make my chest bigger. You'd have to be really vain to do something that drastic. Alison says if bits start to droop or sag as she gets older she'll have them seen to. I wouldn't want her to change her appearance dramatically, but if she'd be happier after surgery, then why not?

9.1

Don't go out without your minder

LEVEL
Elementary

TOPIC
Crime prevention product

ACTIVITY TYPE
Understanding how a gadget works

READING FOCUS
Using illustrations to deduce meaning, extracting key information

TIME
30–40 minutes

KEY LANGUAGE
alarm, battery, cover, key, keyring, pin, ripcord, screw

PREPARATION
One photocopy for each pair of students – cut into four parts (the two pictures, the text and the Exercise); keyring and keys; dictionaries

Warm up

1 Bear in mind that personal attack is a delicate subject and should be treated sensitively. Ask students if the streets of their town or city are dangerous. Have they ever felt in personal danger? Ask students what they would do if they felt in danger.

2 Explain to students that they are going to read a leaflet about something they could use if they were in danger.

Main activity

1 Give each student Picture 1. Ask students to describe what they can see and to say how they think this gadget could help them when in danger. Pre-teach the words *key* and *keyring* using real ones. Do not confirm students' predictions of how the gadget works at this point.

2 Write the word *alarm* on the board. Ask students what an alarm clock does. Explain that the gadget in the picture is a *personal attack alarm.*

3 Give each student Picture 2. Use this picture to pre-teach the other words from Key language. Does this picture confirm students' predictions of how the gadget works?

4 Give each student the text. Ask students to underline the sentence explaining how the gadget works. The answer is in the third sentence.

5 Ask students to continue reading until they find an expression in the leaflet which means *ear-piercing.* (The answer is *extremely loud* in the paragraph headed Warning.)

6 Ask students to continue reading until they find more detailed information about how the gadget works.

7 Ask students to paraphrase the paragraph headed To operate your Minder Alarm.

8 Ask students to look up the word *minder* in their dictionary. (A minder is someone who protects another person, especially a famous person, from danger and unwanted public attention.) Ask them if they think *minder* is a good name for this alarm.

9 Explain that this leaflet is provided with the gadget when you get it. Remind students that it isn't necessary to understand every word in a leaflet such as this. The important thing is to understand how the gadget works.

10 Tell students to imagine that they have bought a *Minder* and that they must answer a friend's questions about it. Give each student the Exercise and ask students to read and find the answers to the questions in pairs.

11 Tell students to change partners. They ask and answer the questions orally together as a role play.

> **Answer key**
> 1 The alarm is extremely loud – 130 decibels of sound. It could cause permanent damage to your hearing.
> 2 The Minder needs three batteries. They last for an hour.
> 3 You can check the batteries by activating the alarm for a short time. Change the batteries when the sound is weak.
> 4 The size of the Minder isn't given in the leaflet – but it is about the same length as a key. You can buy it from JNE Marketing Ltd.
> 5 The alarm is guaranteed for five years – JNE Marketing will change any Minder that is less than five years old if it doesn't work.

Follow up

- Encourage students to find further information about crime prevention products on this and other websites.

Picture 1

Minder

Personal Attack Alarm

Feel secure with a Personal Alarm by your side.

Compact, powerful, efficient, the Personal Alarm is invaluable in all distress situations.

Pull the ripcord for an ear-piercing alarm.

Police and security advisers recommend the use of Personal Alarms to minimise the threat of assault, rape, animal attack and obscene phone calls.

Warning

The effectiveness of the Minder alarm is due to its extremely loud and powerful siren, which produces 130 decibels of sound at source. As a result, prolonged exposure can cause permanent hearing damage.

Do not activate the alarm unnecessarily In particular, take care to avoid endangering small children and pets.

The manufacturer and its agents will not accept any responsibility for any loss, damage or personal injury sustained while in possession of this product whatever the cause or reason.

Power supply

The **Minder** is powered by 3 x LR44 or A76 batteries.

To ensure that your alarm is always at the peak of efficiency, please:

1   Check the batteries' condition regularly by activating the alarm for a short period.
2   At the first sign of a weak sound, replace the batteries with new ones.

To operate your Minder Alarm

Simply pull the cord to remove the pin. The alarm will be activated immediately the pin is removed and will only stop when it is replaced. Minder will run up to one hour on fresh batteries.

To change the batteries in your Minder Alarm

1   Unscrew the Phillips screw on battery cover (picture 2).
2   Remove the cover and replace the batteries, ensuring that the new batteries are inserted as shown in picture 2.

Note: Incorrect insertion of the batteries will prevent your Minder from working properly and will damage the alarm.

3   Replace the screw and re-tighten screw.
4   Always test the alarm after changing the batteries.

Picture 2

Screw

3 x LR44

For inquiries: **JNE MARKETING LTD**.
Tel: 01978-855054
www.jnemarketing.co.uk

Exercise

1   How loud is the alarm? Could this be dangerous?
2   How many batteries does the Minder need? How long do they last?
3   How can you check if the batteries are working? How do you know when to change the batteries?
4   How big is the Minder? Where can you buy it?
5   What happens if the Minder doesn't work?

9.2

Don't forget to pack …

LEVEL
Intermediate

TOPIC
Holiday items

ACTIVITY TYPE
Matching texts with photos

READING FOCUS
Skimming for general sense, identifying main points

TIME
40–50 minutes

KEY LANGUAGE
bank, belt, drawback, pillow, transit

PREPARATION
One photocopy for each pair of students – cut into two parts (the text cut into twelve paragraphs and the photos)

Warm up

1 Begin the lesson by asking students to suggest exotic holiday locations, e.g. The Maldives, Fiji, The Caribbean.

2 Explain to students that they are going to read about and discuss four items that they might take on holiday.

Main activity

1 Divide the class into pairs. Give each pair of students a set of photos. Allow students time to look at the pictures and discuss what the four items are for.

2 Discuss each photo with the class. Get students to describe what they can see and to suggest a name for each item. Guide them towards the names of the items: *Belt Bank, Kepi Hat, Transit Pillow, Bed Specs* and encourage students to suggest why these names were chosen. Write the four names on the board. Ask students if they have used any of these items.

3 Give each pair of students a set of jumbled descriptions. Explain that they have to match the descriptions with the photos. The full name of the item is missing from the first gap in each description. The missing word in each later gap is simply one of these words (*belt, hat, pillow, specs*). They must decide which is the first paragraph of the description for each picture. Point out that it is not necessary to understand every word in the descriptions, just the general sense.

4 Check the answers with the class. The descriptions on the worksheet are with the correct pictures.

5 Tell students to look at the first paragraph of the description for each item and find the item's main selling point. Get them to write a sentence of no more than 15 words for each one. While students are doing this, write the beginning and ending of each of the sentences in Answer key in 6 below on the board.

6 Compare the sentences with the class.

> **Answer key**
> *A Belt Bank has* a thin pocket where you can *store money*. [12]
> *A Kepi Hat has* a curtain around the neck to keep out *the sun's rays*. [15]
> *A Transit Pillow allows* shoulder muscles to relax and you *to sleep on flights*. [14]
> *Bed Specs allow* you to lie flat on your back and *watch television*. [13]

7 Ask students to read the remaining paragraphs for each item and find the item's main drawback(s), if there is one. Ask them to underline the sentences in the paragraphs.

8 Check the answers with the class.

> **Answer key**
> The Belt Bank is not the most stylish belt on the market.
> The only drawback of the Kepi Hat is that you could look like Laurel and Hardy in the 1931 film *Beau Hunks*, when they signed up for the Foreign Legion.
> The only drawback of the Transit Pillow is that it is bulky and weighty (664g).
> The Bed Specs have no drawbacks.

9 Discuss the items with the class. Would students take any of them on holiday? Which one(s)? Why?

Follow up

● Ask students to imagine that they have entered a competition to win a holiday in the exotic location they mentioned earlier. They haven't won first prize, but they have won a runners-up prize – one of the four items in the photos. Students write a paragraph saying which item they would choose, and why. They then write a second paragraph saying why they wouldn't choose the other items.

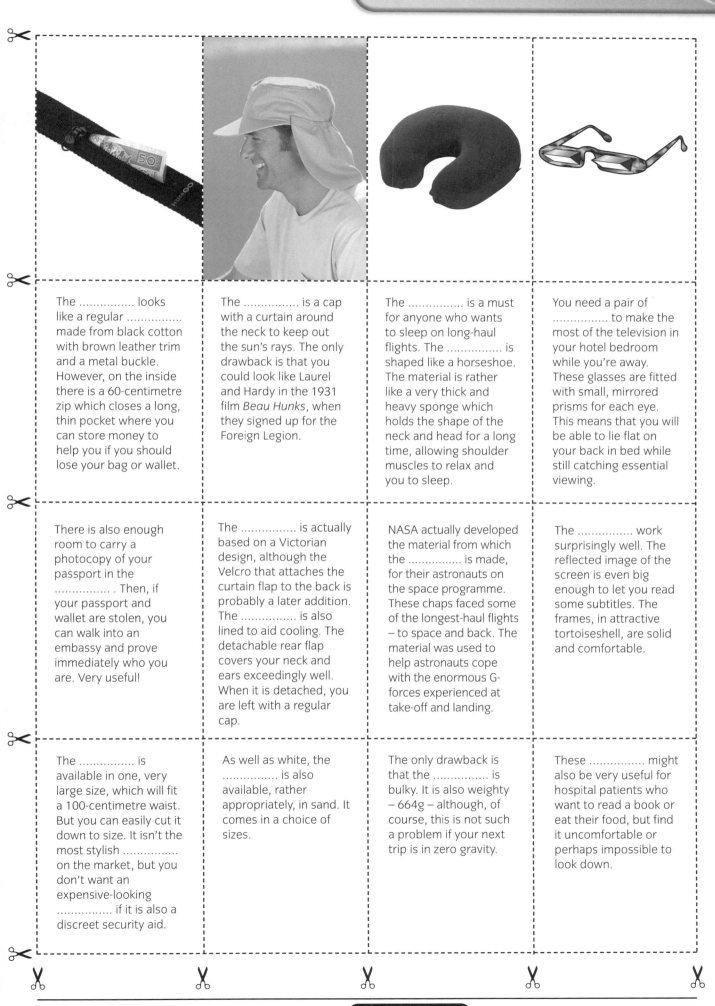

The .... looks like a regular .... made from black cotton with brown leather trim and a metal buckle. However, on the inside there is a 60-centimetre zip which closes a long, thin pocket where you can store money to help you if you should lose your bag or wallet.

The .... is a cap with a curtain around the neck to keep out the sun's rays. The only drawback is that you could look like Laurel and Hardy in the 1931 film *Beau Hunks*, when they signed up for the Foreign Legion.

The .... is a must for anyone who wants to sleep on long-haul flights. The .... is shaped like a horseshoe. The material is rather like a very thick and heavy sponge which holds the shape of the neck and head for a long time, allowing shoulder muscles to relax and you to sleep.

You need a pair of .... to make the most of the television in your hotel bedroom while you're away. These glasses are fitted with small, mirrored prisms for each eye. This means that you will be able to lie flat on your back in bed while still catching essential viewing.

There is also enough room to carry a photocopy of your passport in the .... Then, if your passport and wallet are stolen, you can walk into an embassy and prove immediately who you are. Very useful!

The .... is actually based on a Victorian design, although the Velcro that attaches the curtain flap to the back is probably a later addition. The .... is also lined to aid cooling. The detachable rear flap covers your neck and ears exceedingly well. When it is detached, you are left with a regular cap.

NASA actually developed the material from which the .... is made, for their astronauts on the space programme. These chaps faced some of the longest-haul flights – to space and back. The material was used to help astronauts cope with the enormous G-forces experienced at take-off and landing.

The .... work surprisingly well. The reflected image of the screen is even big enough to let you read some subtitles. The frames, in attractive tortoiseshell, are solid and comfortable.

The .... is available in one, very large size, which will fit a 100-centimetre waist. But you can easily cut it down to size. It isn't the most stylish .... on the market, but you don't want an expensive-looking .... if it is also a discreet security aid.

As well as white, the .... is also available, rather appropriately, in sand. It comes in a choice of sizes.

The only drawback is that the .... is bulky. It is also weighty – 664g – although, of course, this is not such a problem if your next trip is in zero gravity.

These .... might also be very useful for hospital patients who want to read a book or eat their food, but find it uncomfortable or perhaps impossible to look down.

9.3

Can't live without … bananas

Warm up

1 Explain to students that they are going to read a newspaper article about bananas. Elicit that in newspapers there are both news stories and features – articles about particular topics. Elicit that a news story might be about a specific theft of bananas, while a feature might be about the general benefits of eating bananas.

2 Explain that this article appeared in *The Guardian*. It summarises articles from other newspapers. Ask students if they can name any British newspapers.

Main activity

1 Give each student a photocopy. Allow students one minute to find the names of seven newspapers.

2 Check the answers with the class. Point out that in Britain, most daily newspapers have a Sunday equivalent – *Independent / Independent on Sunday, Daily Telegraph / Sunday Telegraph*.

Answer key	
Daily newspapers	**Sunday newspapers**
Independent	Sunday People
Daily Telegraph	Sunday Mirror
Sun	The Observer
	Independent on Sunday

3 Look at the opening paragraph of the text with the class. Explain that *go bananas* is an idiom which means *get angry* or *excited and pleased*. It is probably being used here to say that British people are getting very excited about bananas.

4 Ask students to read the descriptions in Exercise A and match the newspapers with the descriptions. Encourage students to work together in pairs so that they can help each other.

> **Answer key**
> **1** The Observer (paragraphs 3 and 4), Daily Telegraph (paragraph 7)
> **2** Sunday People, Sunday Mirror, The Observer (paragraph 1)
> **3** The Observer, Daily Telegraph, Independent on Sunday (paragraph 2)
> **4** The Observer (paragraph 6)
> **5** Daily Telegraph (paragraphs 7 and 8)
> **6** Independent, Sun (paragraph 5)

5 Ask students to read the text again and decide if the sentences in Exercise B are true or false.

6 Check the answers with the class. Encourage students to justify their answers by referring to the text. Use this opportunity to clarify the meaning of any unknown words and idioms.

> **Answer key**
> **1** true: In short, bananas are healthy and they give you a buzz. (Bananas contain chemicals that stimulate the production of serotonin and dopamine, the same neurotransmitters set off by Prozac and ecstasy.)
> **2** false: We spend more money on bananas than any other supermarket item apart from petrol and lottery tickets. (i.e. more money on bananas than any other food item)
> **3** true: For almost every player, the fruit 'is now considered to be indispensable'.
> **4** false: If you have access to bananas, you must have control of world trade and shipping.
> **5** false: You can't distil it into wine, as you can the grape.
> **6** true: 'Euro rules banning bendy bananas and curvy cucumbers [were] declared illegal in the high court.' (i.e. European laws used to ban bananas that weren't straight)

Follow up

- Explain that the *Sunday People, Sunday Mirror* and *Sun* are *tabloids* (popular newspapers with small pages, more pictures, and short, sensational stories) and *The Observer, Daily Telegraph, Independent on Sunday* and *Independent* are broadsheets (larger newspapers, with more serious and detailed reporting). Ask students if they think the references to the newspapers within the text show this at all.

Can't live without ... bananas

1 "We're going bananas," says the **Sunday People**. "Health conscious Britons will munch their way through 725,000 tonnes of bananas this year." This makes them "the UK's most popular fruit", says the **Sunday Mirror**. "We spend more money on bananas than any other supermarket item apart from petrol and lottery tickets and more than 95% of our households buy them every week," adds **The Observer**. "Bananas are us, it seems."

2 Wimbledon has been doing its bit. For almost every player, the fruit "is now considered to be indispensable for recovery between sets and rallies", says **The Observer**. "It is perfectly suited to the testosterone-driven tennis monkeys, with their temper trantrums, swearing and simian behaviour," says Adam Edwards in the **Daily Telegraph**. Greg Rusedski, notes the **Independent on Sunday**, "turns the folding of half a banana into origami art".

3 The banana is important enough to have its own marketing organisation, the Banana Group. Spokesman Lyndsay Morgan explained the fruit's appeal to **The Observer**: "It is easy to open; it is packed with energy,

fibre and vitamins; it is rich in potassium and low in calories. It is also a first-class hangover cure, stabilises blood pressure and soothes heartburn." Its talents don't end there. She says it is the "perfect food" for weaning babies and "you can even use the skins as garden fertiliser ... It is astonishingly versatile".

4 There is more. The thick skinned, unzippable fruit is a chemical powerhouse on a par with anything dished out by the doctor. "Bananas contain chemicals that stimulate the production of serotonin and dopamine, the same neurotransmitters set off by Prozac and ecstasy," says **The Observer**. "In short, bananas are healthy – and they give you a buzz. It is the ultimate food: ambrosia in a saffron skin."

5 What's more, the banana no longer has to be kept on what the **Independent** calls "the straight and narrow". Last week, "Euro rules banning bendy bananas and curvy cucumbers [were] declared illegal in the high court," said the **Sun**.

6 But there is more to a bent banana than double entendres. You might think of it as a humble fruit, but it has "special economic importance as a symbol of the potency of western capitalism", according to **The Observer**. When the Berlin wall fell, groups of East Germans chanted "hold our hands and take us to banana land" because it "meant freedom at least in terms of middle-class affluence. If you have access to bananas, you must have control of world trade and shipping. And if you do that, things surely cannot be that bad".

7 Britain's favourite fruit has its detractors, however. "How I hate bananas," sighs Adam Edwards. He concedes that they have a certain status as the last thing Elvis Presley ate, that they come in their own "recyclable, disposable container", and that they are "a veritable gourmet support system". And yet: "the banana is not as other fruits – it has never grown up. It is not in the same class as the apple, the orange, the peach, or any other of God's great takeaways." You can't distil it into wine, as you can the grape; you can't use it to reach gastronomic heights.

8 "It remains a juvenile delinquent to be squashed in sandwiches," concludes Edwards, "a one-dish wonder suited only for the palate of a child."

Exercise A

Match the newspapers with the descriptions.

1 remind(s) us of the benefits of eating bananas

2 talk(s) about British banana-buying habits

3 describe(s) banana-eating at the Wimbledon tennis championships

4 talk(s) about a reference to bananas at a historical event

5 compare(s) bananas negatively with other fruit

6 talk(s) about changes in the law with regard to bananas

Exercise B

Decide if these statements are true or false.

1 Bananas, like a drug, can give you a feeling of excitement.

2 British people spend less on bananas than other supermarket food items.

3 Most tennis players at Wimbledon eat a banana during their matches.

4 'Banana land' was a country that didn't trade with the rest of the world.

5 You can make wine from both bananas and grapes.

6 It used to be European law that bananas had to be straight.

10.1

What is a friend?

LEVEL
Elementary

TOPIC
Texts based around
the word *friend(s)*

ACTIVITY TYPE
Reading and
matching

**READING
FOCUS**
Recognising
dictionary
definitions and
separating from
examples, speed-
reading, scanning for
specific words,
skimming for text type

TIME
40–50 minutes

KEY LANGUAGE
*(membership) card,
dictionary entry, friend,
magazine article,
newspaper article,
poem, proverbs,
sayings, website*

PREPARATION
One photocopy for each
student – cut into two
parts (the dictionary entry,
and all the other texts)

Warm up

1 Ask students how they would define the word *friend*. Encourage students' suggestions, but do not confirm their answers at this point.

2 Explain that you want students to read a dictionary entry for *friend* and to compare it with their answer.

Main activity

1 Give each student a dictionary entry. Ask students to check the definition for *friend* and to highlight the meaning so that this is separate from the examples. Elicit that *friend* has two meanings (1 a person whom you like, 2 a person or organisation who helps and supports someone or something). Ask students what other information the dictionary entry gives about the word *friend* (3 a definition of *Friends of the Earth*, 4 some sayings which include the word *friend*). Write the above four points in a list on the board.

2 Explain to students that they are going to look at a variety of different text types in English, which all include the word *friend* or *friends*. Give each student a set of texts. Allow them two minutes to underline or highlight the word *friend(s)* in the texts.

3 Divide the class into pairs. Ask students where they think these texts are from.

4 Check the answers with the class. Write the seven text types in a list and begin to build up a chart on the board.

5 Students read the texts and decide if the word *friend(s)* relates to meaning 1 or meaning 2 on the board.

6 Check the answers with the class. Explain that *proverbs* is another word for *sayings*.

7 Ask students who exactly would read the dictionary definition. Elicit that this could be a student of English, wanting to check which verbs and prepositions to use with *friend(s)*.

8 Students read texts A–G again and decide who exactly would read each text. How and why would they read the text? Would they look at the whole text (skim)? Or would they look only for specific information (scan)?

9 Check the answers with the class. Emphasise the point that in our everyday lives the way we read something depends on the reason why we are reading.

Answer key

text	text type	meaning	readers	reading style
A	newspaper article	1	anyone interested in the news – particularly people from Oxford	1 skim – to find out what happened 2 scan, e.g. for names – if you already know something about the accident
B	story blurb (or reader)	1	student of English	1 skim – to find out about the story 2 scan – to find out author, level, etc.
C	poem	1 (toys, not people)	children, or parents to children	read aloud
D	magazine article	1	children or teenagers	skim – for amusement, and to find out if your experiences are similar
E	proverbs (or sayings)	1	people who are thinking about the nature of friendship	read intensively and reflectively
F	website	2 (and 3)	anyone interested in the work of *Friends of the Earth*	1 skim – to find out what the website offers 2 scan – for a specific icon, for example
G	membership card	2	member, box office staff	1 skim (member) – to find out how to use the card 2 scan (box office staff) – to note card number and expiry date

Follow up

● Ask students to think of other text types in which they might find the word *friend(s)*. Ask them to collect examples before the next lesson.

Oxford woman rescues friend from river
A

A 22-year-old woman was rescued from the Thames on Friday evening. Joelle Parkes, from Osney, fell overboard at Godstow Lock, near Oxford. Rachel Powers, the boat's owner, jumped into the water and rescued Miss Parkes. Both women were taken to the John Radcliffe Hospital, but were later released.

Cambridge English Readers level 3
B

Series editor: Philip Prowse

Just Good Friends
Penny Hancock

It's Stephany and Max's first holiday away together and they want to get to know each other. They go to Italy and stay at Stephany's friend Carlo's flat in a Mediterranean village. But Carlo's wife is not very happy to see Stephany – and the two couples find out why, and a lot of other things about each other, in a hot Italian summer.

Friends
C

I used to feel lonely every night until my father said, "What you need is a special friend you can cuddle in your bed."

First I had a teddy, then I had a dog, then I had a panda, a rabbit and a frog.
Then I had a tiger, a snake and then a bat, a lion and an elephant, a zebra and a cat.

Now my bed is full of friends, but the problem is, you see, though none of them feel lonely there's no room left for me.

friend COMPANION /frend/ n [C] a person whom you know well and whom you like a lot, but who is usually not a member of your family *She's my* **best/oldest/closest** *friend – we've known each other since we were five. He's a* **family** *friend/friend* **of the family**. *We've been friends* (= have liked each other) *for many years. José and Pilar are* **(good)** *friends* **of** *ours* (= we like them). *We're* **(good)** *friends* **with** *José and Pilar. She said that she and Peter were* **just (good)** *friends* (= they were not having a serious or sexual relationship). *Emily has* **made** *friends* **with** (= formed a relationship with and likes) *a new child in her class at school. Now children, can't you* **be** *friends* (= behave in a pleasant way that shows that you like each other) *and play quietly together?* A person or organisation that is a friend **to/of** someone or something helps and supports them: *Thank you for being such a good friend to me, when I had all that trouble. The Friends of* (= The organisation which supports) *the Royal Academy raised £10000 towards the cost of the exhibition*. **Friends of the Earth** is an international organisation which aims to protect the environment. *(saying)* 'With friends like you, who needs enemies' means although you are my friend, you are treating me very badly. *(saying)* 'What are friends for?/That's what friends are for' means that someone has said or done the particular thing they have said or done because they are your friend.

What my friends would change about me
D

Shout **readers reveal what annoys their mates most!**

"They'd change the fact that I'm always late for everything! It's not my fault; my mum's like that too. I try to be on time but something always seems to go wrong, especially when I'm trying to get to school in the morning!" *Basia, London*

"They'd make me go to their school so we could all be together. At the moment I go to a different one across town and I hate it there and miss them." *Eilish, Kent*

E

With a friend at your side, no road seems too long.
JAPANESE PROVERB

Hold a true friend with both your hands.
NIGERIAN PROVERB

One can do without people, but one has need of a friend.
CHINESE PROVERB

A mile walked with a friend contains only a hundred steps.
RUSSIAN PROVERB

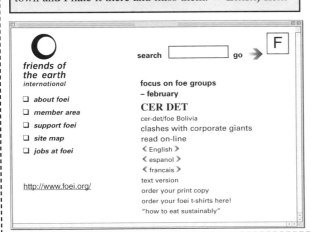

F

friends of the earth
international

search _____ go →

- ❏ about foei
- ❏ member area
- ❏ support foei
- ❏ site map
- ❏ jobs at foei

http://www.foei.org/

focus on foe groups – february
CER DET
cer-det/foe Bolivia
clashes with corporate giants
read on-line
‹ English ›
‹ espanol ›
‹ francais ›
text version
order your print copy
order your foei t-shirts here!
"how to eat sustainably"

Friends Membership Card
THE OXFORD PLAYHOUSE
G

0 0 1 3 6 7 0 1

Expiry date: End 03 / 03

Name(s): Miss E.M. Driscoll

Please quote your membership no. when booking

Box Office: **01865 305305**   THE OXFORD PLAYHOUSE

When booking always ask for your Friends Discount.
Quote your membership number when booking.
Please bring your card with you when collecting tickets.
Your membership card is valid until the expiry date shown on the front.
This card is your receipt and proof of membership – please keep it safe at all times.

10.2

How to make new friends

LEVEL
Intermediate

TOPIC
Ways to meet new people

ACTIVITY TYPE
Note-taking

READING FOCUS
Reading for detail, inferring information from textual clues

TIME
40–50 minutes

KEY LANGUAGE
Present simple, past simple

PREPARATION
One photocopy for each pair of students – cut into two parts (the texts and the Exercise)

Warm up

1   Explain to students that they are going to read about and discuss ways to make new friends outside work or school. Ask students how they met their friends. Also encourage them to suggest other ways to meet new people. Write a list on the board, e.g. *join a club, use public transport.*

Main activity

1   Divide the class into pairs. Give each pair of students the texts. Allow students two minutes to find how many of the suggestions in the list on the board are mentioned in the texts.

2   Discuss the answers with the class. Write a list of suggestions, plus names of the writers, on the board. (See the chart in Answer key below.)

3   Ask students to turn the texts face down on their desks. Make sure students are aware that the four writers are talking about their own personal experiences of making new friends. Ask students to identify what kind of things the writers mentioned, e.g. success/failure, what other people do/suggest, rather than specific experiences.

4   Give each pair of students the Exercise. Add columns 1–4 to the chart on the board. Make sure that students understand that the numbers refer to the questions in the exercise.

5   Tell students to copy the chart on the board. They then read the texts again and complete the chart with information about each writer.

6   Check the answers with the class and complete the chart on the board.

Answer key	1	2	3	4
Kate go to public places enrol in an evening class	yes no	yes —	— yes	— yes
Jonny go to a dating agency answer a personal ad in the paper join a sports club	no yes yes	— no yes	no — —	— — —
Adele go on holiday do voluntary work join a conservation group	yes no yes	yes — yes	— no —	— — —
Tim use Internet chatrooms meet through mutual friends	no yes	— yes	yes —	no —

7   Ask students to read the texts again and to find out if the four writers want to meet new people in general or new people of the opposite sex, or both. Explain that they must also find information in the text to support their decision.

8   Discuss the answers with the class.

> **Answer key**
> **Kate** – both. Her friend from the theatre is female, but Kate implies that if she goes to an evening class next year, she might meet a man and go off on holiday with him.
> **Jonny** – opposite sex. He says he wanted to meet someone special and that he answered the ad because everyone at the bike club was male. People often use a dating agency or personal ad when they want to meet people for a romantic relationship.
> **Adele** – people in general. She says nothing about men. She only talks about meeting lots of people (of all ages).
> **Tim** – both. He says that he's met quite a few people, both male and female, through mutual friends. He also says that he met his girlfriend at a party.

Follow up

• Students write a paragraph about how they met some of their friends.

You want to meet someone special … or simply some new people. What's the best way to make new friends? Write and tell us about your experiences.

I think a good way to meet people is to go to public places, like cafés and galleries, even launderettes. There's always a lot to talk about in a museum, isn't there? And the people are all likely to be interested in the subject matter. I met one of my friends at the theatre. We both had single tickets and sat next to each other. She and I talked about the performance in the interval and then went out for a meal afterwards. Now, we go to the theatre together regularly. Another way to meet people is to enrol in an evening class. My sister joined an Italian class two years ago. Learning a language gives you many opportunities to start a conversation. She started talking to one of the men in her class – and they're off to Italy on holiday together next month! Perhaps I'll join an evening class next year!

Kate, aged 25

I wanted to meet someone special, but I didn't know the best way to do this. I didn't want to go to a dating agency because that could be expensive. So I decided to answer a personal ad in the local paper. I wrote a letter to the girl, then she phoned me. We spoke a couple of times, then we arranged to meet in a pub halfway between our homes. I arrived on time, and waited and waited … That's right, she didn't turn up at all! But I started talking to one of the barmaids and we've become good friends. Another way to meet people is to join a sports club. You can get fit as well as meet people. I joined a mountain-biking club last year – but the other members are all male. That's why I answered the personal ad.

Jonny, aged 23

You can meet people on holiday. I went on a group walking-holiday in Crete last year. The holiday was great, and, it's true, I met lots of people. However, they were all from the south of England and I'm from the north-west. It would be difficult for me to meet up with them very often. I took the plane home to Manchester on my own, and started talking to the girl next to me. We talked about Crete all the way back. We're planning to go back together next year! This girl, Sonia, works for Oxfam. She runs one of their charity shops, and she says they're always looking for volunteers – people to help in the shop. Why didn't I do voluntary work one Saturday a month? I'm more of an outdoor person, so I didn't want to spend all that time indoors. I joined a local conservation group, instead. I've met lots of people of all ages. I also like to think I've helped the environment too!

Adele, aged 22

Internet chatrooms are the newest and easiest way to talk to strangers worldwide. That's what my brother says, and he does it a lot. He chats to people from all over the world. But I don't like the idea of meeting people on the Internet. You hear awful stories about what can happen. Also, I want to meet people locally. I think the best way to meet new people is through mutual friends. So, if a friend of mine offers me the last place in a holiday cottage, invites me to a party or asks me to make up a four for tennis, I jump at the chance! I meet quite a few people, both male and female, this way. And that's how I met my girlfriend – at a friend's party exactly a year ago!

Tim, aged 24

Exercise

1 Did he/she try this way to meet new people?

If the answer is **yes**, go on to question 2.

If the answer is no, go on to question 3.

2 Was he/she successful in meeting new people this way?

If the answer is **yes** or **no**, go on to the next way to meet people.

3 Does he/she talk about someone who met new people this way?

If the answer is **yes**, go on to question 4.

If the answer is **no**, go on to the next way to meet people.

4 Does he/she want to try this way of meeting new people?

If the answer is **yes** or **no**, go on to the next way to meet people.

10.3

LEVEL
Upper-intermediate

TOPIC
Customs and traditions (Easter, getting engaged)

ACTIVITY TYPE
Reading comprehension

READING FOCUS
Extracting key information

TIME
30–40 minutes

KEY LANGUAGE
boyfriend, (prospective) bride, donor, Easter, engaged, fiancé(e), graduate, husband-to-be, plumber, recipient

Past modals: *can't / could / might / must / should / shouldn't / would / wouldn't have*

PREPARATION
One photocopy for each student

Fiancée loses her ring in Easter egg swap

Warm up

1 Explain to students that they are going to read a newspaper article about Easter. Ask them why and how people celebrate Easter. Make sure students are aware that giving chocolate Easter eggs to friends and family is an Easter tradition in some countries.

2 Write the title of the article *Fiancée loses her ring in Easter egg swap* on the board. Elicit or explain that *swap* means *exchange* and a *fiancée* is *a woman who is engaged to be married*.

3 Ask students to suggest what the article is about and what could have happened. Do not confirm students' predictions at this point.

Main activity

1 Give each student a photocopy. Encourage students to work in pairs or small groups on A, so that they can help each other.

> **Answer key**
> 👤 husband-to-be, 30-year-old plumber, donor, fiancé, boyfriend
>
> 👤 fiancée, 26-year-old law graduate, unlucky recipient, prospective bride

2 Ask students to complete the sentences in B, using the text to help them. Check the missing words with the class first. Then ask individual students to read out a sentence each in the correct order.

> **Answer key**
> a He b She c He d He e She f He g She h He
> a 2 b 4 c 8 d 3 e 6 f 7 g 5 h 1

3 Again, encourage students to work in pairs to answer the questions in C.

> **Answer key**
> 1 The man was angry and the woman was upset.
> 2 He hit her.
> 3 She went to see Luca Maori, a Perugia lawyer.
> 4 Because she was thinking about taking legal action against / claiming damages from her boyfriend.
> 5 He isn't optimistic that they will get the ring back.
> 6 He is more optimistic that they will get back together again.

4 Write the following questions in speech bubbles on the board as if they were part of a conversation: *Do you like your new ring? Which ring?* Ask students who might have said these things. Students will probably all agree that the man and woman might have said the things. Then ask how the couple must have felt when they dicovered what had happened.

5 Write the modal verbs from Key language on the board. Encourage students to use the verb forms in sentences about the young couple, e.g. *He shouldn't have hit her, She can't have liked plain chocolate.*

6 Ask students how they would have felt and what they would have done if they had been the young man or woman, e.g. *I wouldn't have swapped the egg, I would have bought a cheaper ring.*

7 Ask students what they would have done if they had found the ring when the egg was resold, e.g. *I'd have taken it back to the shop.*

Follow up

- Students imagine what happened next. They then write the article which appeared in the newspaper the following Sunday (April 22nd). Unfortunately, there was no follow-up article in *The Observer* on Sunday April 22nd, so who knows what happened!

A Read the article. Put the words and phrases under the correct symbol.

Male
👤

....
....
....
....
....

Female
👤

....
....
....
....
....

fiancée   26-year-old law graduate
husband-to-be   30-year-old plumber
donor   unlucky recipient
prospective bride   fiancé   boyfriend

B Complete the sentences with *he* or *she*. Then number the sentences in the order in which they happened.

a .... put the ring inside the egg. ☐

b .... saw that the egg was plain chocolate and decided to exchange it. ☐

c .... went to the shop, but someone else had bought the egg. ☐

d .... gave the other person the egg as an Easter present. ☐

e .... took the egg back to the shop and got a milk chocolate one. ☐

f .... discovered that the other person had exchanged the egg. ☐

g .... didn't know that there was a ring inside the egg. ☐

h .... bought a plain chocolate egg and an engagement ring. ☐

C Answer these questions.

1 What happened when the couple discovered that the ring had been taken back to the shop?

2 How did the young woman get her minor injuries?

3 Who did she go and see?

4 Why have legal papers been prepared?

5 What does Luca Maori think will happen to the ring?

6 What does he think will happen to the young couple's relationship?

Fiancée loses her ring in Easter egg swap

by Philip Willan
Rome

An expensive engagement ring hidden as a surprise in a chocolate Easter egg has given enormous pre-marital tension to a young Italian couple.

The £1,300 ring has gone missing after the fiancée, a 26-year-old law graduate, decided to exchange the plain chocolate egg for a milk chocolate equivalent.

When he discovered what had happened, her husband-to-be, a 30-year-old plumber, rushed back to the shop where he had purchased the egg, only to find that it had already been resold.

The missing ring has put the relationship under considerable stress, with angry words from the donor and tears from the unlucky recipient.

'The episode has caused a lot of tension, even resulting in a very strong slap in the face for the prospective bride,' Luca Maori, a Perugia lawyer said yesterday. 'She contacted me, because she was thinking about taking legal action against her fiancé for her minor physical injuries.'

Maori yesterday made an appeal on television to whoever found a gold ring with a heart-shaped diamond and three rubies in a plain chocolate Easter egg to return it to the shop. There is a handsome reward, he said. 'I have all the legal papers ready to claim damages from the boyfriend, but we will wait for the moment.'

Maori said he was now more optimistic that the couple would stop arguing and get back together again than that they would recover the ring. 'For one thing, the fiancée has promised she will learn to like plain chocolate,' he said.

So far the costly surprise has caused much more disappointment than the plastic toys usually found in chocolate eggs.

11.1

Daily wake-up and warm-up

LEVEL
Elementary

TOPIC
Exercise routine

ACTIVITY TYPE
Following
instructions and
carrying out an
exercise routine

READING FOCUS
Using illustrations to
deduce meaning

TIME
30–40 minutes

KEY LANGUAGE
arms, *back*, *bottom*,
elbows, *feet*, *fingertips*,
hands, *head*, *hips*, *knees*,
neck, *shoulders*, *thighs*,
toes, *tummy*, *waist*

Imperatives

PREPARATION
One photocopy for each
student – cut into seven
parts (the list of exercises
and the six pairs of photos)

Warm up

1 Ask students to name parts of the body. Invite individual students to touch part of their body and say the corresponding word. Write a list on the board. Make sure that you include the words in Key language.

2 Explain to students that they are going to read and carry out an exercise routine. Explain that the exercise routine is part of an authentic text. It hasn't been simplified, but the accompanying pictures will help them to work out what to do.

Main activity

1 Give each student the list of exercises. Get students to read the text and underline the parts of the body that are mentioned in the exercises. Encourage students to compare their answers with a partner.

2 Check the answers with the class. Add any extra words to the list on the board. Make sure that students can all identify these parts of the body.

> **Answer key**
> elbows, feet, knees, fingertips, shoulders, back, arms, neck,
> head, tummy, bottom, hips, toes, hands, waist, thighs

3 Explain to students that they are now going to match a pair of pictures with each exercise. Give each student a set of pictures. Again, students can help each other to match the pictures with the exercises.

4 Check the answers with the class. The pictures on the worksheet opposite are correctly matched with the text.

5 Explain to students that they are now going to do the exercises. Make sure that they don't have any medical conditions or injuries that prevent them from doing certain exercises.

6 Tell students to stand up and make sure that they have enough space to do the exercises. Go through the first exercise with the class as an example. Read out each instruction for students to follow. Break up each sentence into parts, e.g. *Stand tall / with your feet shoulder-width apart / and knees slightly bent*. Demonstrate the actions yourself as you read out the instructions.

7 Tell students to work in pairs. They use the pictures to work out how to do each exercise. Go around the class, helping and demonstrating where necessary.

8 Explain to the class that you want pairs of students to demonstrate an exercise to the rest of the class. The other students must identify the exercise. Point out that they can refer to the text while they are watching a demonstration, but not to the pictures. Tell students to put the pictures away.

9 Ask pairs of students to take turns to demonstrate. The other students say the name of the corresponding exercise.

Follow up

● Students work in pairs and prepare instructions for another exercise. They then take turns to give their instructions to the class. The other students must do the exercise.

Elbow lifts

1 Stand tall with your feet shoulder-width apart and knees slightly bent. Place your fingertips on your shoulders with your elbows close to your body. Raise your elbows straight in front of you and continue to raise them as high as is comfortable.

2 Swing your elbows out to the sides and then back in again. Repeat.

Neck turn

1 Stand comfortably with your back straight and arms relaxed by your sides. Lengthen your neck by lifting the crown of your head towards the ceiling.

2 Turn your head to the left as far as you can comfortably manage. Hold for two seconds. Turn back to the front, pause and repeat on the other side.

Torso twist

1 Stand with your feet shoulder-width apart and knees slightly bent. Pull in your tummy muscles, tuck your bottom underneath you, and fold your arms at shoulder level.

2 Turn the top half of your body to the left as far as you can go, while keeping your hips facing front. Repeat to the right. Alternate until you have completed eight on each side.

Hip swing

1 Stand with your feet slightly wider than hip-width apart. Bend your knees towards your toes. Put your hands on your hips.

2 With your bottom tucked underneath you and both knees equally bent, swing your hips slowly from side to side.

Side bends

1 Stand with your back straight, feet shoulder-width apart, knees slightly bent and hands behind your head.

2 Tucking your bottom underneath you, bend from the waist to the left and then straighten. Repeat to the right.

Squats

1 Place both feet flat on the floor, shoulder-width apart. Look straight ahead.

2 Bend your knees over your toes while bending slightly forwards at the waist. Place your hands on the top of your thighs as you bend to support your back. Return to an upright position.

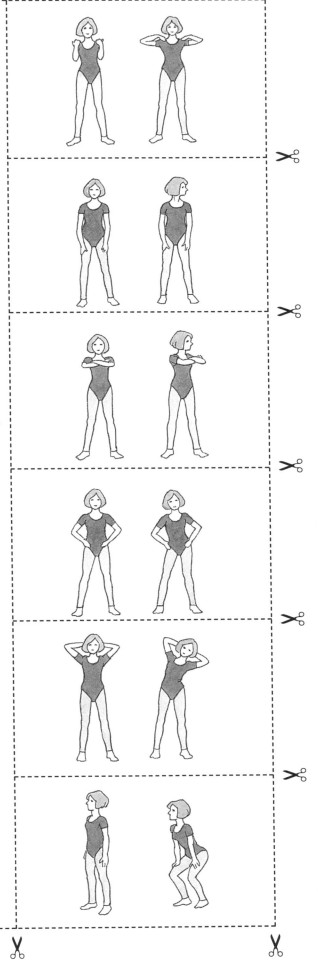

11.2

What shall I do, Doc?

LEVEL
Intermediate

TOPIC
Health jokes

ACTIVITY TYPE
Matching punch lines with joke questions

READING FOCUS
Sentence structure, paraphrasing

TIME
30–40 minutes

KEY LANGUAGE
arm, bone, brain, eye, fingernail, foot, tooth

PREPARATION
One photocopy for each pair of students – cut into two parts (the Questions and the Punch lines, with the Punch lines cut into fifteen strips)

Warm up

1 Begin the lesson by writing the words from Key language on the board. Elicit that these are all parts of the body. Ask students what medical problems you can have with these parts of the body.

2 Explain to students that they are going to read about and discuss medical problems.

Main activity

1 Give each pair of students the list of Questions.

2 Ask students to look at each question in turn and decide who is speaking to whom. Then get them to suggest a reply, e.g. *1 Don't eat so much sugar, 2 I fell off my bike.*

3 Discuss the answers with the class.

> **Answer key**
> 1 patient – doctor   6 friend – friend   11 patient – doctor
> 2 friend – friend   7 patient – doctor   12 pedestrian – pedestrian
> 3 dentist – patient   8 friend – friend   13 patient – doctor
> 4 patient – doctor   9 patient – doctor   14 doctor – patient
> 5 doctor – patient   10 friend – friend   15 patient – doctor

4 Use the jokes below to introduce the idea that the questions are actually the first lines of two-line jokes.

Jokes

1 *'How did the accident happen?'   'My wife fell asleep in the back of the car.'*

2 *'What will you do when you're as big as your mother?'   'Diet.'*

5 Discuss the first question on the photocopy with the class. Ask if anyone can suggest the punch line.

6 Students work in their pairs and predict the punch lines. They write their punch lines in a list.

7 Give each group of students a set of Punch lines. Tell students to match the punch lines with the questions. The punch lines should be ordered as shown on the worksheet.

8 Check the answers with the class.

9 Ask students to paraphrase the punch lines.

> **Suggested answers**
> 1 Don't eat all day.
> 2 I fell over the steps.
> 3 You're hurting my foot.
> 4 I will kill you.
> 5 Because fish have hundreds of bones!
> 6 Meeting my wife was a mistake.
> 7 But you haven't got a pain in your right foot.
> 8 He went out every night.
> 9 You can bite fingernails with teeth, but not cure the habit of biting them.
> 10 He hit a train.
> 11 Tea doesn't give you a pain in the eye.
> 12 A vehicle will hit you, and an ambulance will take you to hospital.
> 13 A car will knock you down.
> 14 Is money more important than health?
> 15 You haven't got a brain.

Follow up

• Ask students which of the jokes they particularly like, and why.

• Encourage students to tell any jokes they know in English.

Punch lines

Questions

1 I'm putting on too much weight. What shall I do, Doc? | Push yourself away from the table three times a day.

2 How did you break your arm? | You see those steps? Well, I didn't.

3 I haven't touched your tooth yet, have I? | No, but you're standing on my foot.

4 Doctor, I often feel like killing myself. What shall I do? | Leave it to me.

5 Does every bone in your body hurt? | Yes, I'm glad I'm not a fish.

6 Have you ever had a car accident? | Well, I met my wife at a petrol station.

7 What do you recommend for the pain in my left foot, Doc? | Try walking with the other one.

8 So Jones is dead. Did he leave his wife much? | Oh, nearly every night.

9 What's good for biting fingernails? | Sharp teeth.

10 How did your brother have his accident? | He tried to fly his plane through a tunnel without checking the train timetable.

11 Why do I get a sharp pain in my left eye every time I drink tea? | Take the spoon out of your cup.

12 What's the quickest way to get to the hospital? | Stand in the middle of this road for a while.

13 What's the best way to stay healthy? | Not to get sick.

14 Could you pay for an operation if I thought one was necessary? | Would you find it necessary, Doc, if I couldn't pay for it?

15 How long can a man live without a brain, Doc? | I don't know. How old are you?

11.3

LEVEL
Upper-intermediate

TOPIC
Skiing down Everest

ACTIVITY TYPE
Understanding an authentic newspaper article

READING FOCUS
Answering your own questions about a text

TIME
40–50 minutes

KEY LANGUAGE
-ing and -ed word endings

PREPARATION
One photocopy for each student

'Insane' daredevil skis down Everest

Warm up

1 Explain to students that they are going to read an article from the British newspaper *The Observer*. The article has not been simplified in any way. It contains lots of words that they may have never met before.

2 Explain that the text is about Mount Everest. Encourage students to say what they know about Mount Everest – facts and figures, and also what they know of the dangers, disasters and deaths there.

Main activity

1 Write the title of the article *'Insane' daredevil skis down Everest* on the board. Elicit or explain the meaning of *insane* (*mentally ill*, although often used informally) and *daredevil* (someone who does dangerous things and takes risks). Write the bi-line *Extreme sports hero slides to a record* on the board. Invite students' comments about the person/story.

2 Ask students what they want to know about this story. Elicit one or two questions, e.g. *Who is the daredevil? How old is he?* Then divide the class into pairs or groups of three. Tell students to write at least ten questions they want the text to answer. As they work, write a few prompts on the board. For example, *weather, feelings, publicity, ascent, alone, money, first mountain, first attempt on Everest.*

3 Get students to read out a question each. Tell other students to add any extra questions to their list.

4 Give each student a photocopy. Students read the text and find answers to their questions in pairs or groups of three.

5 Discuss the answers with the class.

6 Remind students that they can focus on aspects of grammar when reading a text. For example:

   a) Get students to identify words which end in *-ing*. Ask them which words function as nouns. Then get students to rephrase sentences from the text which include the *-ing* form as a verb. For example: *Slovenian Davo Karnicar yesterday became … when he triumphed over … and people who had dismissed him as mad*.

   b) Get students to identify words which end in *-ed*. Ask them which words function as adjectives.

   c) Get students to identify adjectives that appear before nouns, e.g. in the first paragraph: *extreme, treacherous, first*. Then ask which can be omitted from the text. Elicit that most of the adjectives in this text are very strong, and add a lot of colour. It isn't essential to understand their meaning, however.

> **Answer key**
> **a)** nouns – skiing, meaning, thinking
> **b)** *-ed* adjectives – exhausted, exhilarated, peeled, estimated, placed, attached, failed
> **c)** adjectives which can be omitted – extreme, treacherous, dramatic

Follow up

● Encourage students to find further information about Davo Karnicar and his expedition on the website. They can also find out more about Himalayan expeditions on this website: www.everest.com.

'Insane' daredevil skis down Everest

Extreme sports hero slides to a record, reports **Paul Harris**

Triumphing over extreme cold, treacherous ice and people dismissing him as mad, Slovenian Davo Karnicar yesterday became the first person to ski non-stop down Mount Everest.

After a dramatic plummet over almost sheer cliffs of snow, boulders and ice, 38-year-old Karnicar emerged exhausted but exhilarated in his base camp after five hours of skiing that gave new meaning to the words off piste.

At one stage he had to speed over stretches of ice that collapsed and broke underneath him and could have sent him tumbling into the deep crevasses that dot the mountain.

'I feel only absolute happiness and absolute fatigue,' he said after his successful run landed him in the record books and notched another in a series of bizarre firsts of Everest that already includes launching a paraglider from the 8,850-metre summit.

© PAN Advertising Agency

The descent by the father of three had been seen by many as insanely dangerous. The Darwin Awards website, which documents and applauds foolhardy deaths, called the descent 'madness' and urged people to log onto internet broadcasts of the attempt. 'Keep your eyes peeled for a live Darwin Award,' it said.

However, the only body to make news yesterday was a corpse of an unknown mountaineer which Karnicar zipped past as he descended, one of an estimated 120 cadavers, thought to litter the slopes. For Karnicar it was a reminder of the potential perils of his sport, but it did not stop him.

'This mountain is always full of surprises, seeing a dead man out there was a really shocking experience,' he said.

Thanks to strategically placed cameras on the mountain and one attached to his safety helmet, hundreds of thousands of people in more than 70 countries witnessed his descent on the internet. During the run more than 650,000 hits were registered on the expedition website – www.everest.simobil.si – jamming it for a time as others tried to access the site.

Those successful in logging on shared in the drama. At one stage Karnicar prompted deep concern after he failed to radio in to his support team just before he negotiated a notorious outcrop called the Hillary Step. But there had been no disaster. It was just the extreme weather hampering the operation of his radio batteries.

In fact the conditions were so severe that he abandoned plans to rest on the summit before attempting to descend. Instead, suffering from fatigue, as soon as he reached the top he put on his skis and flung himself back down the mountain.

He had already skied down Mont Blanc, the Matterhorn, the Eiger and Annapurna, but Everest was the last great challenge of the extreme side of the skiing world.

Tackling the mountain had already cost Karnica two fingers when a failed attempt saw him get frostbite as a fierce storm lashed the peak.

Karnicar comes from an illustrious skiing family in Slovenia and took part in his first Himalayan skiing expedition in 1989. Since then he has been tireless in raising funds and sponsorship for more expeditions, with Everest as the eventual goal.

'Extreme skiing is my sport, my thinking and life itself,' he said.

12.1

A life of leisure

LEVEL
Elementary

TOPIC
Leisure activities

ACTIVITY TYPE
Authentic everyday texts

READING FOCUS
Speed-reading, identifying text types from visual clues, reading for specific information

TIME
40–50 minutes

KEY LANGUAGE
diary, e-mail, leaflet, programme (cinema, theatre), recipe, ticket, timetable (train), TV listing

PREPARATION
One photocopy for each student – cut into three parts (the texts, Student A's questions and Student B's questions)

Warm up

1   Ask students what they read in their own language in their everyday lives. Write a list of text types on the board, e.g. *newspaper, book, letter, advertisement.* Make sure that the list includes the items in Key language.

2   Explain to students that they are going to look at a variety of different text types in English.

Main activity

1   Give each student a set of texts. Allow them just one minute to look at the seven texts and work out where each text comes from.

2   Check the answers with the class. Write the seven text types in order in a new list on the board. (See Answer key below.)

3   Ask students to look at the seven texts again and identify the exact topic. Ask *What is the recipe for? What is the leaflet about?*, etc.

> **Answer key**
> **A** recipe (for savoury filled pancakes)   **E** TV listing (for Friday night)
> **B** leaflet (about sports centre classes)   **F** cinema programme (for the weekend 6–7 July)
> **C** ticket (for Edward III)   **G** diary
> **D** e-mail (about travel plans)   **H** train timetable (Oxford to London Paddington)

4   Explain to the class that the diary is Jane's diary and that the other texts all relate to Jane's week. Students take the role of Jane.

5   Divide the class into pairs. Give one student in each pair the Student A questions and the other student the Student B questions. Ask students to find the answers to their questions. Partners then take turns to ask each other the questions they have just answered.

6   Check the answers with the class. Point out that these are the type of questions we ask when we read such texts in everyday life.

> **Answer key**
> **Student A: 1** no **2** yes **3** Row A Seat 46 **4** 12.14 **5** Paul **6** 100g **7** 7.00 **8** Wednesday
> **Student B: 1** yes **2** Friday, **3** *The One With The Red Sweater* **4** 9.00 **5** plain
> **6** one hour **7** evening **8** Friday evening

7   Ask students to complete the diary with information from the other texts. Encourage students to work in pairs so that they can help each other.

8   Check the answers with the class.

> **Answer key**
> **1** circuit training   **2** salmon   **3** 17.15   **4** London   **5** Big Brother   **6** Edward
> **7** Ocean's Eleven

Follow up
● Get students to bring as many different types of texts as they can find to the next lesson. Tell them to supply a question for each one. All the students then look at the class selection of texts and questions, and try to answer as many of the questions as they can in 15 minutes.

A

Savoury filled pancakes

Pancakes	Filling
100g plain flour	1 x 215g tin salmon
salt	4 spring onions, chopped
1 egg	600ml white sauce
300ml milk	salt and pepper
oil for frying	100g grated Cheddar cheese

B

FITNESS AT FERRY SPORTS CENTRE 2002
A QUICK GUIDE TO THE FITNESS CLASSES WE OFFER
TO AVOID DISAPPOINTMENT WE RECOMMEND BOOKING IN ADVANCE

MONDAY	9.30 – 10.30 am	MOVE & STRETCH
	5.45 – 6.45 pm	STEP AEROBICS
	7 – 8.00 pm	CIRCUIT TRAINING
TUESDAY	9.30 – 10.30 am	LEGS, BUMS & TUMS
	12 – 12.45 pm	AEROBICS
	6 – 7.00 pm	BODY CONDITIONING

C

SWAN THEATRE
STRATFORD-UPON-AVON

RSC
ROYAL
SHAKESPEARE
COMPANY

EDWARD III
BY WILLIAM SHAKESPEARE

on SATURDAY 6th JULY 2002
at 7.30 PM

GALLERY 1   ROW A Seat 46

D

Hi, Jane! Got your message on Friday.
My coach arrives in Oxford at 17.15 on
Wednesday. You'll meet me, won't you?
See you then!
Love, Gail

E

7.0	**News** Sport, weather
7.30	**Extinct** The Dodo (R) Why did the dodo disappear in the 17th century?
8.30	**Big Brother** Friday Night's Eviction Night with Davina McCall
9.0	**Friends** The One With The Red Sweater
9.30	**Frasier**
10.0	**Big Brother** Davina McCall interrogates the latest loser

F

Phoenix
Picturehouse

Sat 6
Kids' Club: MONSTERS, INC. [U]
   12.00
BEND IT LIKE BECKHAM [12]
   2.00, 9.00
AMADEUS: DIRECTOR'S CUT [PG]
   4.00, 7.30
OCEAN'S ELEVEN [12]
   4.30, 6.45

Sun 7
ABOUT A BOY [12]
   12.00, 2.15
BEND IT LIKE BECKHAM [12]
   2.00, 9.00
AMADEUS: DIRECTOR'S CUT [PG]
   4.30
OCEAN'S ELEVEN [12]
   4.30, 6.45
THE ROYAL TENENBAUMS
   8.0

G

1 JULY   Monday
.... 7.00 (booked)

2 JULY   Tuesday
Paul here for dinner
– buy tin of ....

3 JULY   Wednesday
Meet Gail at ....

4 JULY   Thursday
Off work
– Day in .... with Gail

5 JULY   Friday
Dinner with Mum and Dad
Remember to video
.... (8.30, 10.00)

6 JULY   Saturday
.... III 7.30 pm Stratford

7 JULY   Sunday
.... 6.35
– meet Paul outside cinema

H

Mondays to Fridays			
Oxford		London Paddington	
Oxford	London Paddington	Oxford	London Paddington
0915	1011	1115	1214
0958	1052	1145	1244
1015	1114	1200	1256
1045	1144	1215	1314

Student A

1 Is *The Royal Tenenbaums* showing at the cinema on Friday?
2 Are there any lunchtime fitness classes?
3 Where are you sitting at the Swan Theatre?
4 What time does the 11.15 train get into Paddington?
5 Who's coming for dinner on Tuesday?
6 How much cheese do you need for Savoury filled pancakes?
7 What time is the news?
8 Which day is Gail coming to Oxford?

Student B

1 Can you book fitness classes in advance?
2 When did Gail get your message?
3 Which episode of *Friends* is on TV?
4 What time is *Bend it like Beckham* showing on Saturday evening?
5 What kind of flour do you need for the pancakes?
6 How long does the train journey from Oxford to London take approximately?
7 Is your Stratford ticket for the afternoon or evening?
8 When are you seeing Mum and Dad?

12.2

LEVEL
Intermediate

TOPIC
Photography, film and television

ACTIVITY TYPE
Everyday text (brochure)

READING FOCUS
Reading for specific information

TIME
40–50 minutes

KEY LANGUAGE
Present simple

PREPARATION
One photocopy for each student

The National Museum of Photography, Film and Television

Warm up

1   Ask students if they are interested in photography. Encourage them to talk about their interest in this subject. Then ask if they are interested in film. Finally ask if they are interested in television.

2   Explain to students that they are going to read a brochure for a museum of photography, film and television. Ask if anyone has been to such a museum. Then ask what kind of things they would expect to be able to see and do in such a museum.

3   Tell students that you are planning a trip to the National Museum of Photography, Film and Television in Bradford. Ask them what kind of things they want to know before you go to the museum. Elicit one or two questions, e.g. *Is the museum open on Mondays? How much does it cost?* Then divide the class into pairs. Tell students to write at least ten questions that they want answers to. As they work, write a few prompts on the board. e.g. *café, special exhibition, cinema, children, telephone.*

4   Encourage students to read out a question each. Tell the other students to add any extra questions to their list. Continue until all the class questions have been covered.

Main activity

1   Give each student a photocopy. Ask students to read the text and find answers to their questions. Encourage students to continue working together in pairs so that they can help each other.

2   Ask students to ask and answer the questions across the class.

3   Students continue working together in pairs. They role play a conversation between a receptionist at the museum and someone who has phoned the museum for information.

4   While students are working, write the following words in a list on the board: *animals, history, science and technology, soap operas, cartoons.*

Tell students to imagine that they are particularly interested in the subjects in the list and to find out from the brochure what they should see and do at the museum.

5   Check the answers with the class.

> **Suggested answers**
> animals – Dolphins, Bugs
> history – The Kodak Gallery, Ghosts of the Abyss
> science and technology – Hands-on TV, Space station 3D
> soap operas – TV Heaven
> cartoons – Animation brought to life

Follow up

●   Ask students what they would do and see at the National Museum of Photography, Film and Television. Encourage students to find further information about the museum on its website: www.nmpft.org.uk, if they have access to the Internet.

THE NATIONAL MUSEUM OF PHOTOGRAPHY, FILM & TELEVISION

NMPFT

Bradford, West Yorkshire BD1 1NQ
Enquiries 0870 7010200
Education bookings 0870 7010201
Fax 01274 723155
www.nmpft.org.uk

ADMISSION TO THE MUSEUM IS FREE

OPENING TIMES

Museum	10.00am – 6.00pm
Tuesday – Sunday Bank and school holiday Mondays	
Shop	10.00am – 6.00pm
Café-Restaurant	10.00am – 5.30pm
Pictureville café-bar	5.00pm – 9.00pm
Cinemas	11.00am – late

GALLERIES

A visit to the NMPFT is a great day out. Look back to early television and forward to a virtual world. Here's a taste of some galleries to help you plan your visit.

THE KODAK GALLERY

Trace the history of popular photography, with every camera imaginable – from 19th century glass plate wooden contraptions to today's digital gadgets.

HANDS-ON TV

Operate cameras, read the news, vision-mix or take a magic carpet trip in our TV studios.

NEWS AND BBC STUDIO

Discover how news stories are constructed and presented and think about the effect they have on viewers and society as a whole.

TV HEAVEN

Settle down in front of the box and browse through the best (and the worst) of British TV. Soap, comedy, drama, documentary – the choice is yours!

ANIMATION BROUGHT TO LIFE
Let *Chicken Run* and *Wallace & Gromit* transport you around the world and art of the animator.

EXHIBITION

The temporary exhibition galleries present world-class exhibitions on photography, film, television and new media.

Prices

Prices vary according to exhibition.

Gift vouchers, saver tickets, special group rates and season tickets available.

IMAX CINEMA

With a screen five storeys high showing amazing 3D films, you actually become part of the action.

www.imaxnorth.co.uk

BOX OFFICE

0870 7010200
Standard IMAX films are approximately 40 minutes long.

IMAX prices

Full:	£5.95
Child/concession:	£4.20
Children under 5:	FREE
Group rate:	20% discount

(ten or more people, booked and pre-paid 14 days in advance)

Films change. For latest films see www.imaxnorth.co.uk

SPACE STATION 3D

Suspend yourself in space with the crew of the International Space station as they undertake the most impressive feat since landing a man on the moon.

DOLPHINS

Swim with wild dolphins as you embark on an underwater adventure to find out more about these extraordinary creatures. No wetsuits required!

© Ecoscene

BUGS 3D

Bugs! 3D shrinks you to the size of a fingernail to experience, first hand, an insect's environment. Where raindrops fall like hand grenades, a leaf weighs more than a lorry and blades of grass soar to the clouds like skyscrapers. Visiting this micro-universe, you find yourself immersed in a huge and hostile land where hungry predators stalk prey and fight for survival against the odds.

GHOSTS OF THE ABYSS 3D

Directed by James Cameron, Ghosts of the Abyss will take you on the 3D journey of a lifetime, more than two miles beneath the surface and into the ruined wreck of the great ship Titanic. You will travel to locations unseen for more than ninety years. Through the magic of 3D, you will truly feel as though you are there as they "fly" their amazing equipment through the ship's ruined majesty.

BOND, JAMES BOND

Whether you're a film lover, a Bond fan or simply mad about production and design, Bond, James Bond is an exhibition you must not miss.

Created by the Museum, this remarkable new exhibition celebrates 40 years of the world's best-known movie phenomenon – the James Bond films.

'The Bond, James Bond exhibition is a NMSI touring exhibition curated by the National Museum of Photography, Film, & Television. The exhibition is currently on tour in the USA.'

BOND, JAMES BOND

12.3

Adrenalin capital

LEVEL
Upper-intermediate

TOPIC
Extreme sports

ACTIVITY TYPE
Getting main points
from mini-texts

**READING
FOCUS**
Identifying topic,
paraphrasing,
choosing titles

TIME
40–50 minutes

KEY LANGUAGE
*bungy-jumping,
kayaking, parachuting,
rock climbing,
waterskiing,
white-water rafting*

PREPARATION
One photocopy for
each pair of students;
photos of people doing
extreme sports

Warm up

1 Explain to students that they are going to read about and discuss some extreme sports. Ask students to name as many extreme sports as they can (see Key language). Write a list on the board. Use any photos you have brought to the lesson to elicit the names of sports.

2 Ask students if they have done or would like to do any of these sports.

Main activity

1 Write the title of the article *Adrenalin capital of the world* on the board. Ask students to suggest which city or country the text might be about.

2 Give each pair of students a photocopy. Allow students 30 seconds to identify where the *adrenalin capital* is.

> **Answer key**
> South Africa, rather than any specific city or area of the country

3 Students read the text and identify the extreme sport in each description. While they are working, you can indicate which sports in the list on the board are mentioned.

4 Check the answers with the class. (See Suggested answers below.)

5 Ask students to read the descriptions and work out exactly how to do each sport.

6 Check the answers with the class. Individual students paraphrase a description each without naming the sport. Encourage other students to guess the sport.

> **Suggested answers**
> 1 swimming with sharks: You go in a boat to 'shark alley', a narrow channel between Dyer Island and Geyser Rock. When a shark comes close to the boat, you get into a steel cage, which is lowered into the sea.
> 2 tandem skydiving: You go up to 3,600 metres in a plane. You are tied to your tandem skymaster. Together, you jump out of the plane.
> 3 a walking safari: You follow wild animals on foot with a guide. Your guide has a rifle.
> 4 ballooning: You climb into the basket and balloon over the Magalies Valley to a height of 300 metres.
> 5 quad biking: Quad bikes have thick tyres and automatic gears. They can easily cross rivers and climb steep mountains on the trails around Cape Town and Johannesburg.
> 6 rock climbing: There is lots of fantastic rock climbing about three hours' drive from Johannesburg. There are climbs for everyone – from beginner to expert.
> 7 bungy jumping: A rubber band is attached to your foot. You jump from a great height – 216 metres from the Bloukrans Bridge.
> 8 abseiling: You go to the top of Table Mountain by cable car. At the top, you're attached to ropes. Then you walk backwards off the mountain.
> 9 off-road driving: Off-road driving is driving across country – down mountains and rocky landscapes – where there are no roads.
> 10 whitewater rafting: The water on the Doring River is more exciting than most other rivers for white-water rafting.

7 Discuss snappy titles for the first two descriptions with the class. Combine pairs or groups of three students so that you have a maximum of six larger groups. Students work together and choose snappy titles. Students then vote for the best title, other than their own.

> **Possible titles**
> 1 Jaws – and me   2 Speed, then silence   3 Walking with elephants
> 4 Up and away   5 Bulldog on wheels   6 Adrenalin high   7 Saved by the band
> 8 The long drop   9 Roving off-road   10 Rapid rafting

Follow up

• Ask students which sports in the text are not suitable for people who don't like a) water, b) heights, c) animals, d) driving. Then ask which they think is the most dangerous sport.

> **Answer key**
> **a)** 1, 10   **b)** 2, 4, 6, 7, 8   **c)** 1, 3   **d)** 5, 9

1 _____

A face-to-jaw meeting with a great white is almost a certainty in the Cape's famous 'shark alley', a narrow channel between Dyer Island and Geyser Rock, the breeding ground for jackass penguins and fur seals. Once a great white is spotted, a specially-designed two-man steel cage is lowered into the sea. When the shark is lured close to the boat with tasty pilchard bait, divers can inspect those yawning jaws up close.

2 _____

A s we approached 3,600m tandem master Jeff Bergh was instructing me on our skydive. 'We'll move to the aircraft door on our knees.' (No!) 'I'll swing one leg out of the door' (and because I am tied to him, so will I). 'Bend your head backwards, and then we'll jump!' At first we were travelling at a speed of nearly 200kph. Then, at 1,370m, our parachutes opened and silence filled my mind. I had only one question on landing: 'Can we do it again?'

3 _____

F ollowing a herd of elephants is thrilling enough, but the .458 rifle over your field guide's shoulder will remind you that a walking safari is not only fun and games. You can get as close as 30m to elephant, rhino and buffalo, and even lion.

4 _____

D rifting in an enormous picnic basket on a gentle breeze while watching the sun rise over the Magalies Valley is a much more refined version of adventure. Especially when the pilot cracks open the champagne at 300m.

5 _____

Q uad bikes are a bit like riding a bulldog over rough ground. But with thick tyres and automatic gears, they handle river crossings and steep mountains with ease. There are lots of tracks around Cape Town and Johannesburg, with enough mud, sand and rocky hills to keep the adrenalin flowing.

6 _____

A bout three hours' drive from Johannesburg, on the edge of an escarpment, is a rock climbing nirvana named the Restaurant at the End of the Universe by a Douglas Adams fan. It is a vast landscape scattered with sport crags graded to suit every level of expertise.

7 _____

I t's official. The Guinness Book of Records has declared that the 216m-high Bloukrans Bridge is the highest commercial bungy jump in the world. The countdown to your jump provides the first rush of adrenalin as you stand high above the Tsitsikamma forest. Then comes the jump, attached to just a rubber band. Be prepared for a post-bungy high that lasts for hours, and a strong reminder every time you watch yourself on the video.

8 _____

Z ooming to the top of Table Mountain is on the to-do list of every visitor to Cape Town. You get fantastic views, but it's not exactly an adrelalin rush. But to abseil – walk backwards – off the edge of the mountain from the top, with a drop of 1,000m to the ocean below you … that's exciting. When you're dangling off a rope with nothing below you for a few thousand feet, the view tattoos itself onto your memory in a way a cable car ride never can.

9 _____

T here was a frozen moment as I edged my Land Rover over the side of the mountain and stared at the rocky landscape that was supposed to be a track. But once down, having bounced from rock to rock, exhilaration poured like sweat from my body. Off-road driving is great!

10 _____

T he Doring River runs through the Cedarberg mountains and, in winter, is whiter and more rapid than most. In summer, the Umkomas River picks up speed on its 300km journey from the Drakensberg Mountains in a wilderness area where zebra, bushbuck and the occasional leopard can be seen.

13.1

Cambridge English Readers

LEVEL
Elementary

TOPIC
Using guided readers

ACTIVITY TYPE
Pre-reading activities
(before reading a
reader)

**READING
FOCUS**
Predicting storyline
from cover, blurb,
chapter headings, list
of characters,
illustrations, shadow
reading

TIME
40–50 minutes

KEY LANGUAGE
Present simple, past
simple

PREPARATION
One photocopy for
each student – cut up
into four strips (covers,
words, blurbs and the
chapter headings / the
list of characters / the
illustration / the first
page of text); copies of
Level 1 Cambridge
English Readers *The
Big Picture*, *Help!*, *John
Doe* and *Just Like a
Movie* and tapes (if
available)

Warm up

1   Ask students if they have ever read any stories or books in English. Point out that the best
way to improve their English, and their reading in particular, is to read as much as possible.
Explain that you are going to do some work on graded readers.

Main activity

1   Give each student the top strip of book covers. Discuss each book cover in turn with the
class. Get students to describe what they can see and to predict what the story might be
about. Do not confirm or contradict students' opinions. Explain that *John Doe* is the name
used in an American law court for a person whose real name is kept secret. It is also used
for someone whose identity is not known, or for an average or typical American man.

2   Get students to suggest words that they might expect to find in each story. Again, do not
confirm or contradict their suggestions.

3   Give each student the second strip of words. Ask students to match three words from the
list with each of the book titles. Encourage students to work together in pairs so that they
can help each other.

4   Discuss the answer with the class; but do not confirm or contradict them at this point.
Instead, give each student the third strip of blurbs. Students find the words from the
second strip in the blurbs.

5   Check the answers with the class.

> **Answer key**
> **The Big Picture:** newspaper, photo, sumo star
> **Help!:** computer, stories, writer
> **John Doe:** hospital, name, nothing
> **Just Like a Movie:** movies, girlfriend, real life

6   Point out that they can get a good idea of what a book is about by looking at its front and
back covers. Elicit or explain that they can also use chapter headings, list of characters
(not always available) and illustrations to help predict the content of what they are about
to read and to support them in their reading.

7   Give each student the last strip of chapter headings, the list of characters, the illustration
and the first page of text. Get students to decide which book the chapter headings are
from. They use the chapter headings to predict what might happen in the story. Repeat
this procedure with the list of characters and the illustration. Emphasise the point that
students already know a lot about these stories before they have actually started reading.

8   Students read the opening page of text from *Just Like a Movie*. Ask them a) *Who is 'I' in
this text?* b) *What do you already know about Gina?* Make the point again that students
already know a lot about the story before they actually start reading.

> **Answer key**
> **a)** Brad Black   **b)** She becomes his girlfriend.

Follow up

●   Ask students which of the readers they might like to read. If you have copies of the
readers in a school library, students could take turns to borrow them.

●   Ask students to listen to a section of the tape accompanying the reader book. As they
listen and read, get them to highlight in colour any words or phrases they find particularly
difficult, because of unusual spelling or silent letters. Once students have done this,
encourage them to listen to the tape again and read aloud copying the tape as a model.

  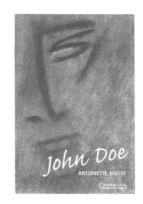 

computer   girlfriend   hospital   movies   name   newspaper
nothing   photo   real life   stories   sumo star   writer

Ken Harada takes photos for newspapers. But life gets dangerous when Ken takes a photo of a sumo star. Someone wants the photo badly. But who? And why?

Frank Wormold is a writer. He doesn't have much money and his wife is unhappy. To help him finish one of his stories he starts to use a computer. But the computer gives him more help than he wants. Then he really needs 'help'!

The man they call John Doe lies in a hospital bed. He watches and thinks but says nothing. The doctor wants to know who he is. But John Doe doesn't answer his questions. Then, after John Doe leaves hospital, the doctor finds out more about him than just his real name.

Brad Black goes to the movies every weekend with his girlfriend, Gina. They are happy, but they have no money. Then Brad has an idea and thinks that real life can be just like the movies – and that's when things go wrong.

Chapter 1 A photo

Chapter 2 Help!

Chapter 3 The key

Chapter 4 Run!

Chapter 5 The police

Chapter 6 The country

Frank Wormold
A writer

Teresa Wormold
A lawyer and Frank's wife

Mel Parks
A Hollywood producer

Chip A computer

A postman

Chapter 1 *Gina*

I love the movies. New movies, old movies. I went to the movies a lot in Toronto. And it all started when I met Gina at the movies.

Gina! We met in October. Four years ago. We met outside a cinema. There was no snow but it was cold. It's cold in Toronto in fall. I was there to buy a ticket for a movie. It was *Forrest Gump*. She was there too, and we started to talk. Just like that.

'Hi,' I said, 'do you live around here?'

'Yes, I do. I live very near here,' she said.

13.2

LEVEL
Intermediate

TOPIC
Teacher's best and
worst day at school

ACTIVITY TYPE
Reading
comprehension

**READING
FOCUS**
Reading for main
message and to
identify writer,
deducing meaning of
unknown words,
paraphrasing,
summarising

TIME
40–50 minutes

KEY LANGUAGE
*arrange, organise,
outing, risk assessment,
swearing, threaten, trip,
victim*

Past simple

PREPARATION
One photocopy for
each pair of students –
cut into three parts
(Text 1, Text 2 and the
Exercises); dictionary

Best day, worst day

Warm up

1 Explain to students that they are going to read about and discuss someone's best and worst day at school. Encourage them to talk about their own best and worst day at school.

Main activity

1 Give each pair of students the two texts. Allow students one minute to decide which text is about someone's best day and which is about their worst day.

2 Check the answers with the class.

> **Answer key**
> Text 1 = best   Text 2 = worst

3 Ask students to read the texts and work out who has written them. Make sure that everyone understands that they have been written by a teacher.

4 Discuss with students what they can do when they come across unknown words in a text. Encourage them to try and work out the meaning of the words from context, and to only use a dictionary as a last resort. Explain to students that they are going to do three exercises which focus on working out the meaning of unknown words in the texts.

5 Give each pair of students the Exercises. Students choose the correct definition for the four words and phrases in A.

6 In B students match four more words and phrases with the other definitions in A.

7 Point out to students that they will often find words with similar meanings in a text. Ask them to find, for example, similar words in the first text for *trip* (*outing*) and *arrange* (*organise*).

8 Ask students to discuss in their pairs the meanings of the four words in C. Do not check their answers at this point. Let them find words in the second paragraph with a similar meaning.

> **Answer key**
> **A** 1 B 2 A 3 A 4 A
> **B** 1 cause accidents, 2 allocated, 3 relaxed, 4 proud
> **C** 1 problem, 2 group, 3 using bad language, 4 warnings

9 Ask students to explain in their own words the following phrases: a) *I imposed my authority*, b) *the victim / the victimised boy*, c) *I enjoy a challenge and will not be defeated*.

> **Answer key**
> **a)** I showed them who was in control
> **b)** the boy who was under attack
> **c)** I like being tested and will not let the situation beat me

10 Ask students to summarise the two experiences in D in their own words. They then complete the summary of each experience with one word in each gap.

11 Check the answers with the class.

> **Answer key**
> 1 first 2 arranged/organised 3 risk 4 prepared 5 behaviour 6 great
> 7 threats 8 thought 9 attempted 10 victim 11 sent 12 exhausted

Follow up

● Ask students if they have considered becoming a teacher. Why? / Why not?

Text 1

My .... day was a school trip to the Forest of Dean Sculpture Trail. As I had never arranged a trip before, I worked closely with the Year 4 teacher to learn from her what I needed to do.

I remembered from my time at university that you had to do a risk assessment before a trip. This meant visiting the sculpture park and noting anything that may cause accidents – for example, steep hills or streams.

Doing the research meant my colleague and I knew what to expect and felt fully prepared. There were 52 children on the trip – they were split into groups of four and five, and each group was allocated an adult.

My class can be a difficult group and I was worried about their behaviour on this trip. But the day was really great – we came back totally relaxed. The children were brilliant, enjoying every part of the day, and we were really proud of them.

I learned a lot from my colleague and I can confidently say now that I could organise a school outing on my own.

Text 2

My .... day happened when I was with a class of 11-year-olds and there was trouble with a gang of boys. They were swearing and making threats to another boy in the class. They thought he was a 'swot' – he worked too hard.

At this point, I imposed my authority – I may be just 1 metre 60, but I can really shout – and the group of boys who had been causing the problem stopped. I gave the whole class some warnings of my own. But later, the victim hit one of the boys who had been using bad language. I attempted to separate them, but the victimised boy started to have a problem with his breathing and began to cough.

By this point, I was really stressed and unsure what to do, so I sent the child next door to calm down. At the end of the day, I came away from that class mentally exhausted.

But the experience has not put me off. It was just a bad day and most teachers get those. So do children. In any case, I enjoy a challenge and will not be defeated.

Exercises

A Find these words or phrases in the first text. Choose the correct definition.

1 do a risk assessment (paragraph 2)
   A be the reason why injuries happen
   B form an opinion about the dangers

2 split (paragraph 3)
   A divided into two or more parts
   B given to someone as their share

3 worried (paragraph 4)
   A anxious or unhappy
   B calm and free from stress

4 brilliant (paragraph 4)
   A very good, fantastic
   B satisfied with what has happened

B Look at each other definition in Exercise A. Find another word or phrase in the same paragraph which matches this definition.

C Find these words in the first paragraph of the second text. What do you think they mean? Find words in the second paragraph with a similar meaning.

1 trouble   2 gang   3 swearing   4 threats

D Complete the summaries with words from the text.

My best day was my (1) .... school trip, which I (2) .... with a colleague. After doing a (3) .... assessment, we felt fully (4) .... My class's (5) .... was brilliant and the day was really (6) ....

My worst day was when a group of 11-year-old boys made (7) .... to a boy they (8) .... was a 'swot'. I (9) .... to separate the (10) .... and one of the gang, and (11) .... him next door to calm down. I was mentally (12) .... at the end of the day.

13.3

Bacon, ham and eggs

LEVEL
Upper-intermediate

TOPIC
Part of a *Just William* story

ACTIVITY TYPE
Ordering a dialogue-based story

READING FOCUS
Text organisation, deducing meaning of unknown words

TIME
40–50 minutes

KEY LANGUAGE
Past tenses, direct speech, adverbs of manner

PREPARATION
One photocopy for each pair of students – cut into ten parts

Warm up

1 Write *Bacon, ham and eggs* on the board. Explain to students that they are going to read a text with this title. Ask students what they think the text is going to be about. (They might well think it is about food and breakfast.) Explain that bacon and ham are both salted or smoked pig, but that bacon is from the back and sides, and ham is from the leg or shoulder. Bacon and ham are similar, but not the same.

2 Write the following words from the first section of the text on the board: *class, lecturer, audience, Shakespeare*. Explain to the class that these words are from the text. Ask students again what they think the text is going to be about. (It is in fact about education and an English lesson.)

Main activity

1 Give each pair of students the jumbled story. Tell them to put the sections of the story in order. When they have done this, they can compare their order with another pair.

2 Check the order with the class. Read aloud the sections in order: down the left column, then the right. Stress all the words *in italics*.

3 Ask students to discuss in their pairs where the title *Bacon, ham and eggs* comes from.

> **Answer key**
> Mr Welbecker mentions Bacon, which William confuses with Ham. William then refers to this Bacon/Ham man as Eggs. When Mr Welbecker mentions Hamlet, William is confused. Mr Welbecker had said he was called Bacon and now he's calling him Ham(let). In the end, William suggests that they say Eggs for both Bacon and Ham(let), then they won't get confused.

4 Students now discuss William's problem with the storyline of the play *Hamlet*. Elicit that William is confused by the use of *his* in the sentence *This man was called Hamlet and his uncle had killed his father because he wanted to marry his mother*. In all three cases *his* refers to Hamlet, but *he* refers to the uncle.

5 Use the Notes below to provide background information when appropriate.

6 Ask students what kind of boy William is. What is it like being one of his teachers?

7 Write *He did it _____ly* on the board. Ask students to suggest adverbs of manner to complete the phrase, e.g. *carefully, slowly*.

8 Ask students to read the text again and underline six adverbs of manner ending in *ly*. Use questions to direct students towards the meaning of the adverbs, e.g. *section 1: Do you think the lecturer wanted to return to William?* (no), *section 2: Was William very pleased that he had asked a question?* (yes).

> **Answer key**
> *reluctantly* [section 1], *triumphantly* [section 2], *dejectedly, politely* [section 6], *irritably, confidingly* [section 10].

Follow up

● Students read out the dialogue between William and Mr Welbecker in pairs. Encourage them to stress the words in *italics* and to read in the manner suggested by the six adverbs.

> **Notes**
> **William** (William Brown) schoolboy hero of short stories. This extract is from *William the Pirate* (1933).
> **William Shakespeare** (1564–1616) The world's most performed playwright.
> **Hamlet** (c. 1601) Shakespearean tragedy.
> **Francis Bacon** (1561–1626) Politician, author and philosopher of science.

Most of the class had by now settled down to their own devices – quiet or otherwise. William was the only one who seemed to be taking any interest in the lecture or the lecturer.

'Well,' said Mr Welbecker, assuming his lecturer's manner, gazing round at his audience, and returning at last reluctantly to William, 'I repeat that I incline to the theory that the plays of Shakespeare were written by Bacon.'

'How could they be?' said William.

'I've already said that I wished you wouldn't keep interrupting,' snapped the lecturer.

'That *was* a question,' said William triumphantly. 'You can't say that wasn't a question, and you said we could ask questions. How could that other man Ham–'

'I said Bacon.'

'Well, it's nearly the same,' said William. 'Well, how could this man Bacon write them if Shakespeare wrote them?'

'Ah, but you see I don't believe that Shakespeare did write them,' said Mr Welbecker mysteriously.

'Well, why's he got his name printed on all the books then?' said William. 'He must've told the printers he did, or they wouldn't put his name on, an' he ought to know. An' if this other man Eggs–'

'I said Bacon,' snapped Mr Welbecker again.

'Well, Bacon then,' said William, 'well, if this man Bacon wrote them, they wouldn't put this man Shakespeare's name on the books. They wouldn't be allowed to. They'd get put in prison for it. The only way he could have done it was by poisoning this man Shakespeare and then stealing his plays. That's what I'd have done, anyway, if I'd been him, and I'd wanted to say I'd written them.'

'That's all nonsense,' said Mr Welbecker sharply. 'Of course I'm willing to admit that it's an open question.' Then returning to his breezy manner and making an unsuccessful attempt to enlarge his audience: 'Now, boys, I want you all to please listen to me–'

No one responded.

Dejectedly Mr Welbecker returned to his sole auditor.

'I want first to tell you the story of the play of which you are all going to act a scene for the shield that I am presenting,' he said. 'There was a man called Hamlet–'

'You just said he was called Bacon,' said William.

'I did *not* say he was called Bacon,' snapped Mr Welbecker.

'Yes, 'scuse me, you did,' said William politely. 'When I called him Ham, you said it was Bacon, and now you're calling him Ham yourself.'

'This was a different man,' said Mr Welbecker. '*Listen!* This man was called Hamlet and his uncle had killed his father because he wanted to marry his mother.'

'What did he want to marry his mother for?' said William. 'I've never heard of anyone wanting to marry their mother.'

'It was *Hamlet's* mother he wanted to marry.'

'Oh, that man that you think wrote the plays.'

'No, that was Bacon.'

'You said it was Ham a minute ago. Whenever I say it's Bacon, you say it's Ham, and whenever I say it's Ham, you say it's Bacon. I don't think you know which his name was.'

'Will you *listen*!' said the distraught lecturer. 'This man Hamlet decided to kill his uncle.'

'Why?'

'I've told you. Because his uncle had killed his father.'

'Whose father?'

'*Hamlet's*. There's a beautiful girl in the play called Ophelia, and Hamlet had once wanted to marry her.'

'You just said he wanted to marry his mother.'

'I did not. I wish you'd listen. Then he went mad, and this girl fell into the river. It was supposed to be an accident, but probably–'

'He pushed her in,' supplied William.

'*Who* pushed her in?' demanded Mr Welbecker irritably.

'I thought you were going to say that that man Bacon pushed her in.'

'*Hamlet*, you mean.'

'I tell you what,' said William confidingly, 'let's say Eggs for both of them. Then we shan't get so muddled. Eggs means whichever of them it was.'

14.1

Start your own business

LEVEL
Elementary

TOPIC
Being your own boss

ACTIVITY TYPE
Read-and-do

READING FOCUS
Identifying topic area, recognising main ideas, intensive reading

TIME
40–50 minutes

KEY LANGUAGE
administrator, competitor, customer, entrepreneur, experience, knowledge, manager, products, qualifications, salesperson, services, skills, training

PREPARATION
One photocopy for each student – cut into four parts

Warm up

1 Write the words from Key language on the board in random order. Tell students that they are going to read a text which includes these words. Ask what they think the text will be about.

> **Answer key**
> work / jobs / business

2 Ask students to put the words into three groups: people and jobs, what businesses sell, what you need to do a job. Encourage them to use a dictionary when necessary. Check the answers with the class.

> **Answer key**
> **people and jobs** – administrator, competitor, customer, entrepreneur, manager, salesperson
> **what businesses sell** – products, services
> **what you need to do a job** – experience, knowledge, qualifications, skills, training

3 Explain that students are going to read parts of a brochure produced by Shell LiveWIRE, one of the UK's community investment programmes. LiveWIRE aims to encourage young people to consider starting a business of their own.

4 Divide the class into pairs. Allow students three minutes to list as many reasons as they can why people might want to be their own boss, and the advantages and disadvantages of working for yourself.

Main activity

1 Give each student How was it for you? Tell students to read the interview and to find the answers to these questions: *What business did Ronan start? Why did he want to be his own boss? What does he say about the advantages and disadvantages of working for yourself?*

2 Check the answers with the class. Encourage students to use their own words rather than simply repeating Ronan's words.

3 Ask students *What kind of person might start their own business and enjoy working on their own? What kind of skills do you need?*

4 Give each student Is starting a business for me? Tell students to read the list of skills and decide which skills they have. Again, encourage students to work in pairs so that they can help each other with any unknown words.

5 Remind students that Ronan set up his own tour company. Ask students to suggest other business ideas, e.g. cooking, secretarial work, language teaching, computer support, bike repairs, dog-walking.

6 Tell students that you want them to think about a business they could start. Give each student What could I do? Get students to work on their own and make notes.

7 Ask students to work in pairs and tell each other about the business they might set up.

8 Give each student Will it work? Students work in their pairs and use the questions to discuss each other's business.

Follow up

● Ask students if they know anyone who has started their own business. How do these people find working on their own?

● Encourage students to find further information about LiveWire on its website: www.shell-livewire.org.

How was it for you?

Ronan McNamara (24) runs McNamara Tours, providing fun and informative tours of Derry City and some of Northern Ireland's best known tourist attractions.

Why did you decide to start your own business?

It had always been my dream. When an opportunity arose, I had to go for it.

How did you develop your business idea?

I spotted a gap in the market for a local private tour operator whilst working for the City Council. I ignored those who told me I was mad relying on tourists visiting Northern Ireland!

What help/advice did you receive?

My local business agency put me in touch with Shell LiveWIRE. My adviser helped me develop my idea, conduct market research, create a business plan and helped me gain financial assistance.

What are the main advantages of being your own boss?

You learn about business fast! You don't have to answer to anyone (except the Bank Manager!) and it's far more rewarding than working for someone else.

What are the worst aspects?

You have to be prepared for long hours – your social life can suffer!

What advice would you offer to other young people thinking of starting their own business?

Get as much advice as you can – but remember it's you that has to make the final decision.

What could I do?

Use a pen and large sheet of paper to write down all of your ideas. It doesn't matter how crazy your thoughts may seem, write anything that comes into your mind as you work through the following sections. You'll be amazed with how many ideas you come up with!

What could you do? Ask yourself:

- Have I a hobby or interest which could be the basis for a business?
- What skills have I got?
- What work have I done?
- What knowledge or experience have I gained?
- Could I adapt my existing skills and work for myself instead of someone else?

Can you spot a new idea?

- identify any opportunities for new products or services
- provide products or services which would overcome difficulties I or people in my area experience
- ask local businesses or organisations which products or services they have difficulty in obtaining

Tried and tested – could you:

- look at an existing business in a new way?
- copy someone else's idea – make it better?
- supply goods or services to local organisations which are currently supplied from outside your area?
- buy an existing business?

Is starting a business for me?

You don't have to be a certain type of person or have particular qualifications to start a business. It takes a mix of qualities to succeed, almost like being several people at the same time. Here are some skills which may be needed to run a business. Which skills do you think you might have?

- **Manager** responsible, decision maker, leader, planner
- **Salesperson** winning customers, understanding people, knowing how to talk to them, winning confidence
- **Worker** as you're unlikely to have any employees to start off with, could you do all the work yourself – cope with long hours and pressure?
- **Administrator** keeping accounts, organising paperwork
- **Learner** keeping an open mind and always prepared to learn
- **Thinker** coming up with bright ideas, problem solving
- **Entrepreneur** identifying new business opportunities, wanting to succeed, taking calculated risks

Different businesses require different balances of these skills. If you're lacking in a particular area, you can get support from a specialist adviser. You may be able to get training to gain the skills you think you need. If you have one or more business partners, you should agree who does what best.

Will it work?

Remember – you need to make a living out of your idea! You may find it helpful to talk this through with a friend. Consider:

- What is the aim of my business?
- What product or service will I sell?
- Who are my potential customers?
- What raw materials do I need?
- Where will I base my business?
- What equipment will I need?
- What price will I charge?
- How will I find my customers?
- How will I make them buy from me instead of my competitors?

14.2

It's a risky business

LEVEL
Intermediate

TOPIC
Work-related risks

ACTIVITY TYPE
Matching related
paragraphs

**READING
FOCUS**
Intensive reading,
checking predictions

TIME
40–50 minutes

KEY LANGUAGE
*average, chance, curry,
explanation, risk*

PREPARATION
One photocopy for
each pair of students –
cut into two (the
Explanations and Risks
cut into eight strips)

Warm up

1 Explain to students that they are going to read about and discuss some work-related risks. Point out that they might like to take these into account before they consider working in Britain or the USA!

Main activity

1 Give each pair or group of students the list of Risks.

2 Look at the first risk with the class. Make sure that students understand that *curry* is an Indian dish, and that Indian restaurants and takeaways are very popular in Britain. Get students to predict the missing number.

3 Students work in their pairs or groups and predict the missing numbers. They complete the gap in each risk.

4 When students have made their predictions, explain that you are not going to check the answers together. Instead, they are going to match each risk with its explanation and check their predictions themselves.

5 Give each pair or group a set of Explanations. Tell students to match the Risks with the Explanations. They then use the information in the explanations to check their predictions.

6 Check the answers with the class. Get individual students to read out a risk each. Did anyone get all the answers right?

> **Answer key**
> **A** 3 (curry = 70,000 people; steel, ships, coal = about $\frac{1}{3}$ each x 70,000 people)
> **B** 2 (206,000 accountants / 97,500 doctors = 2 accountants / 1 doctor)
> **C** 30 (life span of 80 ÷ 2.7 = 1 in 29.63)
> **D** 100 (14 in 1000 = 1.4 in 100)
> **E** 60 (risk for cab driver = 6 x police driver x 10 x national average)
> **F** 7 (20÷3 = 6 $\frac{2}{3}$)
> **G** 4 (60% x 10, i.e. 6, don't last; 40%, i.e. 4, last)
> **H** 20 (1 in 20 = 5 in 100; 2 in 100 = murders, 2 in 100 = murdered and dumped, 1 in 100 = bath kills a dying person)

Follow up

• Discuss the risks and explanations with the class. Which do students find most surprising / least surprising? Have students been in any of these situations? Do they know anyone who has?

Explanations

Risks

A In Britain, you are .... times more likely to earn your living making curry than making steel, building ships or mining coal.

The 'curry industry' in Britain employs 70,000 people, more than 1 in 300 of the total workforce, and more than the steel, shipping and coal-mining industries put together.

B If you are ill on the train into work, there is a .... in 3 chance that the person opposite is an accountant and not a doctor.

There are 206,000 accountants and only 97,500 doctors in the UK.

C The chances of being in the bathroom when the boss rings up to speak to you are around 1 in ....

The average person spends 3.5% of their life (2.7 years) using the toilet.

D The chances are between 1 and 2 in .... that you will end up in hospital at least once in your lifetime due to a pen, pencil or similar office item.

One in 5,000 Americans a year are injured severely enough by 'desk accessories' to need emergency-room treatment. This translates to a 14 in 1,000 lifetime chance of at least one office-related injury.

E Next time you get into a cab, spare a thought for the driver. For taxi drivers the risk of getting murdered on the job is .... times above the average.

Over 4 in every 10,000 US cab drivers are killed while working. That is over 6 times the risk for police officers, which is itself 10 times higher than the national average.

F If twenty people work in your office, then around .... of them will buy a Christmas gift for the boss. Are you one of them?

Roughly 1 in 3 British employees buy presents for their bosses. So, if your colleague at the next desk hasn't, maybe you should rush out and buy something?

G Have you thought of looking for romance at work? Did you know that nearly .... in ten relationships that begin at work are long-lasting?

Yes, that's right. 60% of couples who meet at work won't stay together for very long – but the rest will!

H Relax after a hard day at the office by taking a bath. And just consider that if you're going to be found dead in the bath, there is only a one in .... chance that it's been murder.

In fact, only 1 in 50 bath-time fatalities are actually murders. The same number again are murdered and then dumped in the bath, while 1 in 100 are only put into the bath to ensure that death occurs.

14.3

Work, sweet work

Warm up

1 Ask students about their jobs and where they work. What are the pluses and minuses of their jobs and companies? Encourage students to talk about the work environment itself. If they don't work, encourage them to talk about imaginary environments. Write + and – symbols on the board and make notes under each heading. Write the following phrases (all from paragraph 1) on the board: *bubbling stream, desperate-looking cactus, dodgy old fridge, dress-down policy, in-house bar, a suit and tie*. Ask students to identify these as plus or minus features.

2 Ask students if they know the expression *Home, sweet home*. This was the title of a song written by the American songwriter J.H.Payne in 1823. The song says *There's no place like home* – meaning that home is a wonderful place.

3 Explain to students that they are going to read a text with the title *Work, sweet work*. Ask them what they think the text is going to be about.

> **Answer key**
> The text is about wonderful work environments.

Main activity

1 Give each student the text. Read out the bi-line under the title. Ask students if they correctly predicted the topic of the text.

2 Allow students one minute to look at the text and decide how many and which paragraphs refer to work environments in general and which paragraphs refer to specific work environments. Elicit the names of the companies.

3 Ask students to read the first three paragraphs in pairs and find two more plus features and two more minus features.

> **Answer key**
> work environments in general – 4: 1, 2, 3, 8
> specific work environments – 4: 4, 5, 6, 7
> companies – St Luke's, Origin Products, Cabal Communications, BA (British Airways)
> plus features – pubs, chill out areas
> minus features – drab meeting rooms, out-of-order coffee machines

4 Write *If employees' work surroundings are better* … on the board. Ask students to read the first three paragraphs again and find two ways of completing the sentence.

> **Suggested answers**
> If employees' work surroundings are better, their work performance is better.
> If employees' work surroundings are better, they may prefer to spend less time at home in future.

5 Give each student the Exercise. Ask students to match the companies with the descriptions. Then discuss with the class what other features the companies offer.

> **Answer key**
> **1** St Luke's   **2** Cabal Communications   **3** BA   **4** St Luke's
> **5** Origin Products   **6** BA   **7** St Luke's   **8** Origin Products

6 Ask students which company they'd prefer to work for and why. Are there any drawbacks?

7 Tell students to read the final paragraph. Ask a) *Does the article end on a serious or humorous note?* b) *Does the writer want an 'office bedroom'?* c) *How do we know this?*

> **Answer key**
> **a)** humorous   **b)** no   **c)** the paragraph ends with an exclamation mark

Follow up

● In pairs or groups students plan a fantastic or awful work environment. They take turns to present their company to the class. Students vote for the best and worst work place.

Work, sweet work

Some companies are cherishing their employees like never before, creating the kind of workplace that you may never want to leave …

Is the only good thing about your office the dodgy old fridge in what is laughingly referred to as the kitchen? Are you still wearing a suit and tie on Fridays? Is the only vegetation in your office a rather desperate-looking cactus? If the answer to these questions is yes, you need to move jobs, preferably to an office with a permanent dress-down policy, an in-house bar and a bubbling stream in the foyer.

Some employers are cherishing their employees as never before. If trends continue, our much-maligned places of work could become venues we actively look forward to being in, and our domestic environment – with difficult partners, screaming kids, rubbish TV and endless bills – could become the place we choose to avoid.

Companies around the country are starting to realise that employees who actually enjoy their work surroundings are likely to perform better too, and are making changes to help make this happen. Pubs and 'chill out' areas are appearing in place of the drab meeting rooms and out-of-order coffee machines we're used to, while perks are getting more and more inventive.

Take the advertising agency St Luke's. This was founded as a co-operative; everyone in the company, whatever position they hold, owns an equal share. And the office is run along the same lines. You can work anywhere: the in-house café, on the sofa, or at any hot-desk available throughout the five floors of open-plan space. At the café you can lunch on subsidised pub food while listening to tunes from the café jukebox. Yoga and t'ai chi classes are paid for by the company, and the Culture Club organises weekly trips to exhibitions. You also get the chance to take part in the 'Make yourself more interesting' scheme. People have used the fund to go scuba diving, learn massage and even how to drive … 'We're currently buying a holiday home, somewhere in the sun but easily accessible, that will be available to all co-owners at a low rate. This must be fairly rare if not unique!' says Belinda Archer from St Luke's. The result? An energetic atmosphere in which company loyalty leads to better performance and service.

Toy-design company Origin Products is moving in the same direction. Everyone gathers around a large table to enjoy a free lunch. There's a state-of-the-art sound system, with a large CD library covering everything from Eminem to Mozart. In the summer, staff take turns to have Friday afternoons off.

But the best thing about a job must be not going to work at all. Companies like magazine publisher Cabal Communications have introduced mental health days, or 'duvet days'. These are really legalised sick days, intended to release pressure in the work environment. You simply phone and tell your boss that you can't face a day at work and, hey presto, you're free to spend the day in your dressing gown watching *Oprah* and reruns of *Quincy* – that will get you back to work as soon as possible!

The recently-opened BA headquarters at Heathrow represents the cutting edge of the modern, user-friendly office block. The building is intended to be a covered microcosm of a city – only without the pollution and the pavement rage. At the centre of the development is a cobbled street with olive trees and a stream. There are shops, cafés and a supermarket. At one end is a restaurant overlooking a tranquil lake, and bridges criss-cross the street, linking the various offices. There's hardly any reason to leave the work environment at all …

So things are moving on from the occasional staff outing and a bit of corporate art on the walls. What will companies have to offer potential employees in the future? When the builders start creating an 'office bedroom' for late night workers, you'll know things have gone just a little too far!

Exercise

Which company does these things? Complete the sentences.

1 .... offers its staff relaxation and exercise classes.
2 .... allows its employees to take a day off work.
3 .... offers its staff a variety of places to eat.
4 .... encourages its employees to learn new things and improve themselves.
5 .... gives each member of staff the occasional long weekend.
6 .... encourages its employees to do their shopping.
7 .... will soon be able to offer its staff cheap holidays.
8 .... encourages its employees to eat together.

15.1

LEVEL
Elementary

TOPIC
Shopping to excess

ACTIVITY TYPE
Matching beginnings and endings of humorous sentences

READING FOCUS
Sentence structure, paraphrasing

TIME
40–50 minutes

KEY LANGUAGE
bill, guarantee, insurance, sales assistant, till receipt, shopaholic, window display

PREPARATION
One photocopy for each pair of students – cut into two parts (the Beginnings and the Endings, with the Endings cut into sixteen strips)

You know you're a shopaholic when …

Warm up

1   Explain to students that they are going to read about and discuss shopping. Get students to suggest words associated with shopping, e.g. *shopping centre, shopping trip.* Make sure all the words in Key language are covered too.

2   Introduce the word *shopaholic.* Explain that you can combine *aholic* with words like *shop, chocolate, work* to describe someone who is unable to stop doing or taking something, i.e. *shopaholic, chocaholic, workaholic.* Ask students if they are shopaholics or if they know anyone who is a shopaholic. Ask them to describe the symptoms or behaviour of a shopaholic.

3   Explain that students are going to read some humorous sentences about being a shopaholic.

Main activity

1   Give each pair or group of students the sentence Beginnings.

2   Encourage students to predict what word or what kind of word may come next. In sentence 1, for example, the next word is most likely to be an article (*a/an, the*), or the pronoun *when*.

3   Students work in their pairs and predict the endings of the sentences. They write their endings in a list.

4   Give each pair or group of students the set of Endings. Tell students to match the endings with the beginnings. Go around the class and help with any unknown vocabulary while students are working.

5   Check the answers with the class. Get individual students to read out a full sentence each.

6   Ask students to paraphrase the quotations.

> **Suggested answers**
> 1 You don't want to relax on a beach, for example; you just want to go shopping.
> 2 Your till receipts are very, very long, because you have spent so much.
> 3 You may have a lot of clothes in your wardrobe, but you still need to buy something for the office party.
> 4 You watch the adverts because they tell you about new things you can buy.
> 5 You have so many things to look at when you're shopping that you have to hurry.
> 6 You spend a long, long time at the shopping centre. (You don't buy very much, however, if your car park bill is more than your shopping!)
> 7 Your friends can think of nothing to buy you.
> 8 You have more free time to go shopping. (But also less money to spend!)
> 9 The school authorities are not as keen on shopping as you.
> 10 Your shopping trips are very, very long.
> 11 You go to the shop so often that you know a lot about the clothes there.
> 12 You prefer to buy something new than get it mended when it breaks.
> 13 If there are matching sets, you will always buy all the parts – even if you only really want one of them.
> 14 You take up new hobbies as an excuse to buy more new things.
> 15 You are so busy trying to look at the things in a shop window that you don't look at the road and nearly have an accident.
> 16 You can justify buying two of something because one of them might break.

Follow up

●   Discuss the sentences with the class. Which do students particularly like? Even if they're not shopaholics themselves, do any of the sentences relate to their own experiences? Are any of their own endings better than the originals?

●   Students make a list of English words that they come across when they are out shopping.

Beginnings

Endings

1 Your ideal holiday is ...

a shopping trip to New York.

2 Your till receipts are ...

longer than toilet rolls.

3 You have a wardrobe full of clothes, ...

but nothing to wear for the office party.

4 You pay more attention to the adverts ...

than to the actual programmes on TV.

5 You never take your partner shopping with you; ...

he'd (she'd) only slow you down.

6 You spend so long at the shopping centre, ...

your car park bill is more than your shopping.

7 You realise you're impossible to buy presents for because ...

you've already got everything.

8 You go part-time at work so that ...

you can spend more time shopping.

9 You attend a school reunion and are shocked that ...

they haven't changed the curtains in the hall since you left.

10 Your average shopping trip takes ...

longer than most people's annual holiday.

11 You know more about the clothes in your favourite shop ...

than the sales assistants.

12 You don't believe in insurance or guarantees; ...

if it breaks, get a new one.

13 You never buy a new toothbrush ...

without getting all the matching dental accessories – toothpaste, dental floss, toothpicks, mouthwash and chewing gum.

14 You take up a new hobby every month so that ...

you can buy a whole new set of essential equipment.

15 You almost crash the car ...

trying to look at a new window display.

16 You buy two of everything; ...

perhaps the first one will break.

15.2

LEVEL
Intermediate

TOPIC
Giving and receiving
presents

ACTIVITY TYPE
Note-taking

**READING
FOCUS**
Recognising main
ideas, reading
'between the lines'

TIME
30–40 minutes

KEY LANGUAGE
Past tenses

PREPARATION
One photocopy for
each student

The best and worst … present

Warm up

1   Explain to students that they are going to read about and discuss presents. Ask when they receive presents. Encourage them to talk about the best and worst presents they have ever received, and given.

2   Ask students what makes a good and a bad present. Use the reasons in Answer key below to guide them. Do not worry, however, if they do not mention all of the reasons.

3   Explain that they are going to read about the experiences of four people. Ask students not to predict exactly what the people will say, but to predict the kind of thing they will say. Use the first four headings in the chart in Answer key below to guide them. Build up the headings and names into a chart on the board as you discuss what the people will say.

Main activity

1   Give each student a photocopy. Tell students to copy the first four columns of the chart on the board and complete them with *yes* when appropriate. Encourage students to work together in pairs so that they can help each other.

2   Explain to the class that the four names are both men's and women's names. (Lee = name for both male and female. Alex = name for both, or short for Alexander [male] and Alexandra [female], Charlie = familiar name for Charles [male] and sometimes for Charlotte [female], Chris = short for Christopher [male] and Christine [female]). Ask students to read the text again and work out if the people are male or female.

3   Elicit that Charlie (clue: *a long dress*) and Chris (clue: *my husband*) are female, and Lee (clue: *her son*) and Alex (clue: *my girlfriend*) are male. Then check the answers and complete the first four columns of the chart on the board.

4   Ask students to read the text again and find occasions when four of the presents were given/received.

5   Ask students to work out the reasons why the presents are good or bad. Get them to refer to the list of reasons they discussed earlier, and to include any reasons they did not discuss.

Answer key						
	best you've received	worst you've received	best you've given	worst you've given	occasion	reason
Lee	yes			yes	birthday	The giver shows they understand the receiver. The giver gives something that they like.
Alex			yes	yes	taking exams	The giver doesn't know the receiver's likes and dislikes. The giver has made a financial sacrifice.
Charlie		yes	yes		foreign business trip	The giver wants to change the receiver in some way. The giver has put a lot of thought into the present.
Chris	yes	yes			wedding anniversary	The giver has made an emotional sacrifice. The receiver has already got the present.

Follow up
●   Ask students if they have had any similar experiences to those they have read about.
●   Ask students what would be the best and worst birthday present they could receive.

What's the best present you've ever received – and the best you've ever given? And what's the worst? Write and tell us about your experiences. There'll be a present for the best letter!

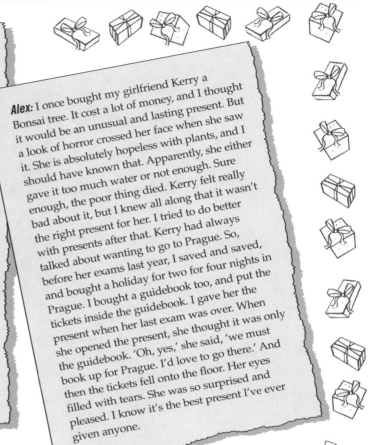

Lee: My mum never goes to the theatre, but she knows I like going a lot. For my birthday, she gave me theatre vouchers – I could use them to buy tickets to a show of my choice. Anyway, I decided to invite her to come along with me, perhaps she would get to like it. So, I got two tickets for Benefactors. Neil Pearson, who she's seen a lot on TV and likes, was in it. She said she would go, but only if she paid for a meal before the show. And she chose a Japanese restaurant. She had never had Japanese food before, but she knew that her son loved it! We had a great evening! From the best … to the worst. I once gave my dad a book that I had read and loved. It was called In cold blood and was a true story about the murder of a family in America in the 1950s. I realise now that it was just not his kind of thing – ever since then he's always asked me to buy him the latest fantasy book by Terry Pratchet or Philip Pullman. I've lost my copy of In cold blood, and sometimes I think I should ask him if I can have his. I'm sure I've given other presents that have not been right, but that's one I know about.

Alex: I once bought my girlfriend Kerry a Bonsai tree. It cost a lot of money, and I thought it would be an unusual and lasting present. But a look of horror crossed her face when she saw it. She is absolutely hopeless with plants, and I should have known that. Apparently, she either gave it too much water or not enough. Sure enough, the poor thing died. Kerry felt really bad about it, but I knew all along that it wasn't the right present for her. I tried to do better with presents after that. Kerry had always talked about wanting to go to Prague. So, before her exams last year, I saved and saved, and bought a holiday for two for four nights in Prague. I bought a guidebook too, and put the tickets inside the guidebook. I gave her the present when her last exam was over. When she opened the present, she thought it was only the guidebook. 'Oh, yes,' she said, 'we must book up for Prague. I'd love to go there.' And then the tickets fell onto the floor. Her eyes filled with tears. She was so surprised and pleased. I know it's the best present I've ever given anyone.

Charlie: I usually wear jeans, tracksuit bottoms, trainers, T-shirts, that sort of thing. And, as far as I knew, my partner Marcus was happy with that. So I got a bit of a shock, to be honest, when he bought me a long dress back from a foreign business trip. I don't wear long dresses, so this must mean that that's what he wants me to wear. I was a bit annoyed too, I'd shown him the new pair of trainers I wanted lots of times. I'm sure he could have got them abroad. The best present I think I ever gave was to someone I worked with. We didn't have much money in those days, but I really took a lot of care with her present. I wrapped a box in beautiful paper, and then filled it with lots of small things. There was a packet of paper hankies – she had a cold at the time; batteries for her alarm clock – she was sometimes late for work; a bar of her favourite chocolate; a comb; even a pair of tights. They say 'It's the thought that counts'. And it's true, I'd put more thought than money into the present.

Chris: The best present I ever had was something I didn't expect at all. My husband and I are both Arsenal supporters, but we've never been to a match. The tickets are impossible to get, and they're too expensive for us. Anyway, one of my colleagues is a season-ticket holder. And last year, for our tenth wedding anniversary, he gave us his tickets for the Arsenal – Manchester United game. That was an amazing thing for him to do. The worst birthday present I ever received was also connected with football. It was a book called Football's strangest matches. I love football, that wasn't the problem. The problem was that I already had the book, and the same person had given it to me the year before! I should have said something at the time, but I was too polite.

15.3

LEVEL
Upper-intermediate

TOPIC
The biggest gold
nugget found in
Scotland

ACTIVITY TYPE
Understanding an
authentic newspaper
article

**READING
FOCUS**
Extracting key
information, creating
questions based on a
text

TIME
30–40 minutes

KEY LANGUAGE
*carat, flake, gold rush,
mining, nugget, pan,
prospector*

PREPARATION
One photocopy for
each student

Gold fever

Warm up

1 Explain to students that they are going to read an article about gold. Get students to say what they know about gold. What is it? Where is it found? What is it used for? Make sure all the words in Key language are covered too.

2 Explain that the article is from the British newspaper *The Guardian*. The article has not been simplified in any way. Remind students to use their knowledge of the topic and find synonyms within the text in order to deal with any unknown words.

Main activity

1 Write the title of the article *Hopefuls head for the hills as gold fever hits* on the board. Ask students what they think the article will be about. Do not confirm their predictions at this point. Instead write the bi-line, one word at a time, under the title. As you write each word, encourage students to predict the next word and invite their comments.

2 Explain that the bi-line summarises the main points of the article. Divide the bi-line into three parts – *Biggest Scottish find in 50 years / awakens worldwide interest in prospecting / around former mining village known as God's treasure house*. Give each student a photocopy. Ask students to read the article and find out what information it gives about each part of the bi-line. Encourage them to use three different coloured highlighter pens to identify the information for each part.

3 Encourage students to work in pairs when they have finished reading so that they can discuss and compare the information they have found.

4 Discuss the answers with the class. Ask students if they think the bi-line is a good summary of the article.

> **Answer key**
> **Biggest Scottish find in 50 years**
> A 6.1g nugget was found by George Patterson, in a stream near Wanlockhead, in June 2002. This was the biggest find for more than half a century.
>
> **awakens worldwide interest in prospecting**
> The find has created a gold rush. The curator of the Scottish Mining Museum says it has been amazing since news of the find went around the world. People have been phoning and asking what they need to do to start (gold panning). The number of people wanting to take the gold panning courses that John Whitworth runs from the museum have gone up five or six times.
>
> **around former mining village known as God's treasure house**
> The former (lead) mining village of Wanlockhead is in the Lowther hills, one of Scotland's most productive gold fields. Gold was first discovered there in the 13th century, and in medieval times the area became known as 'God's treasure house in Scotland', so rich were the pickings.

5 Divide the class into two groups. Explain that the students in one group have to imagine that they are interviewing John Whitworth and the students in the other group have to imagine that they are interviewing George Paterson. They write ten questions for their interview, using the information given in the article. For example, both groups could ask *How old are you? How long have you been panning in the Lowthers?*

6 Divide the class into pairs so that each student is working with someone from the other group. Students interview each other in a role play.

Follow up

• Ask students if they would be interested in panning for gold. Encourage them to find further information about the courses at Wanlockhead on the website: http://www.leadminingmuseum.co.uk.

HOPEFULS HEAD FOR THE HILLS AS GOLD FEVER HITS

Biggest Scottish find in 50 years awakens worldwide interest in prospecting around former mining village known as God's treasure house

Hopeful prospector learns to pan for gold on Menock water near Wanlockhead, Scotland

John Whitworth lowers a shallow plastic pan into muddy water from a small burn deep in Scotland's Lowther hills, sluicing the container back and forward with a practised hand.

"You give it a really good shake then tip your pan forward and back, forward and back and each time it takes a little bit of the stones and silt out. Look, see," he says as small, burnished flakes start to emerge from the layer of mud on the bottom. The small group around him crowds in excitedly. Gold.

"The purest and rarest in the world," says John, scooping up the precious 22.8 carat scrapings with a fingertip and dropping them into a small vial of water where they sink immediately. Whitworth is a gold panning instructor and he has been busy of late, ever since his fellow prospector, George Paterson, found a 6.1g nugget of gold last month in one of the many small streams that slice across this area of the southern uplands.

Paterson's find was the biggest in Scotland for more than half a century and it has created a gold rush as amateur prospectors head for the hills and the courses John Whitworth runs from the Scottish Mining Museum at Wanlockhead.

The former mining village, the highest settlement in Scotland, sits at the heart of one of Scotland's most productive gold fields. It was monks from Newbattle Abbey in Midlothian who first discovered gold in the Lowther hills in the 13th century. In medieval times the area became known as "God's treasure house in Scotland", so rich were the pickings. In 1502 a nugget weighing 2.5lbs was found and it was gold from the Lowthers that was used to fashion the Scottish crown jewels.

The men who worked the lead mines that sprang up in the area in the 1700s panned for gold in their spare time, and it is said the wives of Wanlockhead all wore gold wedding rings, unusual for the age.

With the mines' decline, panning slipped into quiet obscurity, a pastime only for the committed few.

"Gold panning is something that has rumbled along quite happily," said museum curator Rosi Parkes. "But after George Paterson found his nugget and the news went around the world it has been amazing. People have been phoning, asking what they need to do to start, and the number of people wanting to take the courses John runs has gone up five or six times. There is gold taken out every day and bigger pieces found recently."

John Whitworth has panned in the Lowthers for 14 years. In a carved wooden box, glass vials hold the bounty the 59-year-old has recovered – scores of gold nuggets and flakes in various sizes. "I got these all from different streams," he says. "I've never added up all the weight. I think it would scare me too much." His biggest find was a 4.8g nugget, a prize only bettered by George Paterson.

It was in early June that Paterson, who only took up panning three years ago after moving to the area, stumbled across his treasure. At first he thought he had scooped up a rough yellow stone. "I had just started and I saw it lying there. It didn't move like the other stones. I picked it up and when I felt the weight of it, I knew what it was." The small, misshapen kernel could be worth up to £1,000 but Paterson, 48, will not sell it.

"To make it into something would ruin it," he says. "Then it would be only a little bit of gold. The interest is in the nugget. It has been lying there for millions of years. I would never sell any of them. Every one is unique. I can tell you exactly where I got each one. You can never replace them."

Paterson is bemused by the reaction to his find, but not too concerned about the increased competition it has brought. Like other seasoned gold panners he has favourite hunting grounds which he keeps a jealously guarded secret.

"There is a bit of an art to it," he said. "You have got to be able to read the river, the way the river flows. On a bend, it lays the gold down on the slow flowing side. If there is a rock in the river and the river is coming down it, the gold is in front of the rock."

"A lot of people get gold fever. They get so hungry. To me it is just a hobby. But it is compulsive. You are always looking for a bigger and bigger piece."

There are tales of a nugget the size of a horse's head which was discovered by a miner in the 1800s, but was too heavy for him to carry home. He had a heart attack before he could reveal its exact location. There are also rumours of nuggets as big as a man's fist just waiting to be found.

John Whitworth takes the legends with a pinch of salt, but once he has dispensed his advice for the would-be prospectors, he will take his own pan out to the remote locations that he has found over the years.

"Each winter it seems to replenish itself," he said. "You can pan a stretch of river and can go back and there will be more in the same spot. There are other big nuggets to be found. There is gold out there."

16.1

Home and dry

LEVEL
Elementary

TOPIC
A man's amazing achievement

ACTIVITY TYPE
Reading comprehension of an authentic newspaper article

READING FOCUS
Reading for detail, extracting key information, reading between the lines

TIME
30–40 minutes

KEY LANGUAGE
diver's suit, helmet, home and dry, marathon

Past tenses

PREPARATION
One photocopy for each student – cut into three parts (the photo, the text and the Exercise)

Warm up

1   Give each student the photo. Ask them what the man is wearing. Elicit or pre-teach *diver's suit* and *helmet*. Ask students when such outfits were worn. What do they think it is like wearing such a suit? Why do they think the man is in an old fashioned diver's suit?

Main activity

1   Give each student the text. Allow students two minutes to read the text and find the answers to the following questions: a) *Who is the man?*, b) *What exactly is he wearing?*, and c) *Why is he standing under a clock?* Encourage students to work together in pairs so that they can help each other.

2   Check the answers with the class. Use this opportunity to clarify the meaning of any unknown words. Also explain that the title of the article *Home and dry* is an idiom which means to have completed something successfully. It is particularly apt when used to talk about someone wearing a diver's suit.

> **Answer key**
> **a)** Lloyd Scott
> **b)** a rubberised canvas 1940s suit, copper helmet and lead-lined boots
> **c)** He has just finished the London marathon.

3   Give each student the exercise. Ask students to read the text and complete the sentences. Point out that all the missing words are in the text.

4   Check answers with the class. Encourage students to justify their answer by referring to the text. Again, use this opportunity to clarify the meaning of any unknown words.

> **Answer key**
> **1** five: Five days after the London marathon (paragraph 1)
> **2** last: the moment in the Mall when he became the last person to complete this year's race (paragraph 2)
> **3** cancer: When I was diagnosed with cancer … I have come through it (paragraph 3)
> **4** woman: he was welcomed by Paula Radcliffe, who won the woman's race on Sunday (paragraph 4)
> **5** helmet: My biggest fear has been tripping up because I also have very limited vision (paragraph 4)
> **6** firefighter: the former firefighter said (paragraph 4)
> **7** morning: But the hardest thing has been getting started each morning (paragraph 5)
> **8** hard: You cannot imagine how hard it is getting into the cold, wet diving suit with all your muscles still cold and having to think about what lies ahead (paragraph 5)
> **9** raise: hopes to raise £100,000 for the charity Cancer and Leukaemia In Childhood (paragraph 6)
> **10** endurance: is no stranger to extraordinary feats of endurance (paragraph 6)

5   Discuss Lloyd Scott's feat with the class. Ask, for example: a) *Why do you think he didn't simply run like everyone else?* b) *Does it surprise you that he used to be a firefighter?* c) *Why do you think he crossed the Jordan desert, climbed Everest and walked to the South Pole?*

> **Answer key**
> **a)** perhaps because a five-day run would get more publicity and more people would see him
> **b)** probably not – firefighters are always helping other people
> **c)** probably to raise money for charity

Follow up

•   Ask students if they know anyone who has completed a marathon. Do they know anyone who has raised money for charity in other ways? How did they do it?

Home and dry

Jeevan Vasagar

Deep-sea diver finally finishes the London marathon

Five days after the London marathon, when the ordeal was just memory and muscle ache for every other runner, Lloyd Scott lumbered across the finish line in his deep-sea diver's suit to a hero's welcome yesterday.

He called the moment in the Mall when he became the last person to complete this year's race "the most emotional of my life".

"When I was diagnosed with cancer, I needed to know it was not the end," said Mr Scott, 40, from Rainham, Essex. "I have come through it and I hope that this run will inspire anyone else diagnosed not to give up hope."

As he crossed the finish line after five days, 29 minutes and 46 seconds he was welcomed by Paula Radcliffe, who won the woman's race on Sunday. His run, wearing a rubberised canvas 1940s suit, copper helmet and lead-lined boots, had been every bit as hard as he had expected. "My boots weigh a ton and I am very top-heavy. My biggest fear has been tripping up because I also have very limited vision and cannot see kerbs or broken paving stones," the former firefighter said.

"But the hardest thing has been getting started each morning. When I wake up, I have to assess my aches and pains to find out what hurts and how much. You cannot imagine how hard it is getting into the cold, wet diving suit with all your muscles still cold and having to think about what lies ahead."

Mr Scott, who hopes to raise £100,000 for the charity Cancer and Leukaemia In Childhood, is no stranger to extraordinary feats of endurance, having run across the Jordan desert dressed as Indiana Jones, climbed Everest and walked to the South Pole, pulling sledges himself.

Exercise

Complete the statements so that they are true for Lloyd Scott.

1 He finished the London marathon .... days after all the other runners.

2 He finished .... and recorded the slowest time for a marathon.

3 He has had .... and recovered from it.

4 He met the race's fastest .... in the Mall at the end of the race.

5 He couldn't see very well because he was wearing a ....

6 He used to be a .... before he became ill.

7 He didn't walk 24 hours a day, but started the marathon every ....

8 He was in pain during the race and found it very ....

9 He did the marathon to .... money for sick children.

10 He has done three other amazing feats of ....

16.2

James Cook, navigator

LEVEL
Intermediate

TOPIC
Captain James Cook

ACTIVITY TYPE
Matching texts with visuals

READING FOCUS
Scanning for specific words, skimming to identify source, recognising main ideas, note-taking

TIME
40–50 minutes

KEY LANGUAGE
apprentice, artist, farm labourer, grocer, navigator, shipowner

Past simple

PREPARATION
One photocopy for each group of three students – with the heading *James Cook, navigator 16.2* cut off and then cut into six parts

Warm up

1 Revise and/or pre-teach the job words in Key language. Write the word *artist* on the board. Elicit the meaning of *artist*. Repeat this procedure with the other words in the list. Deal with *apprentice* last. Explain that these words are all in the text students are going to read.

Main activity

1 Divide the class into groups of three. Give each student in the group a different text. Allow them two minutes to find the five jobs in the texts. As students are working, write *James Cook, British _____* on the board. Ask students a) which of the words best describes Cook . Then ask them b) if any other jobs are mentioned in the texts and complete the sentences.

> **Answer key**
> **a)** navigator   **b)** teachers, coach drivers

2 Give each group of students the three maps. Ask them to match the maps with the texts. Ask students where the texts have come from.

> **Answer key**
> **A** brochure   **B** encyclopaedia   **C** guidebook

3 Get students to identify in the text who had the five jobs. Again, encourage students to look at one text each, but to show their partners the information they have found.

4 Check the answers with the class. Get individual students each to say something about a job.

> **Answer key**
> Cook's father was a farm labourer.
> Cook's master in Staithes was a grocer.
> James Cook was a ship's apprentice.
> John Walker was a shipowner and Cook's master.
> Cook was a famous British navigator.
> Webber was the artist on Cook's third voyage.

5 As students are working, write the headings in the chart in Answer key below on the board.

6 Tell students to complete the chart with biographical information about James Cook. Discuss the first row of the chart as an example with the class. Point out to students that they will need to combine the information from all three sources to build up a complete biography.

> **Answer key**
>
> | When | What happened | Where |
> | --- | --- | --- |
> | October 27, 1728 | James Cook was born | Marton |
> | 1736–1740 | went to school | Great Ayton |
> | 1740–1745 | helped his father on the farm | Great Ayton |
> | 1745 | worked for a grocer | Staithes |
> | 1746 | became a ship's apprentice | Whitby |
> | 1746–1755 | lived with Captain John Walker | Whitby (Newcastle → London) |
> | 1755 | joined the navy | London |
> | 1759 | became master of his own ship | London |
> | 1762 | married Elizabeth Betts | London |
> | 1768–1771 | first expedition to the Pacific | New Zealand, Australia |
> | 1772–1775 | second expedition to the Pacific | Antarctic Circle |
> | 1776–1779 | third expedition to the Pacific | Hawaii, Canada |
> | 1779 | he was killed | Hawaii |

Follow up

- Encourage students to find further information about James Cook on these websites: www.cookmuseumwhitby.co.uk, www.ycc.org.uk and www.captaincook.org.uk.

A Captain Cook Memorial Museum, Whitby
The house on the harbour, window on the world

Visit the house in Grape Lane where 18-year-old James Cook came as a ship's apprentice. The handsome 17th century house close by the harbour was where Cook's master, the shipowner, Captain John Walker and his family lived. Cook lived here when not aboard Walker's coal ships sailing between Newcastle and London, both during and after his training. The house is Cook's only known home in Whitby, and is now The Captain Cook Memorial Museum. The museum celebrates Cook's nine years in Whitby and the great navigator's three voyages of discovery.

Open	23rd March to 31st October – Daily 9.45 am to 5.00 pm (last admission 4.30 pm)
Admission	Adult £2.80 Child £1.80 Senior Citizen (60+) £2.30 School group £1.50 per child (pre-booked) Accompanying teachers and coach drivers free
Facilities	Special exhibition; gift shop; souvenir guide

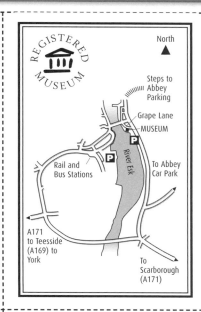

B James Cook (1728–1779) famous for exploring the Pacific and mapping its islands. The son of a farm labourer, Cook worked for a grocer in Staithes for eighteen months before beginning his ship's apprenticeship. In 1755 he left Whitby, and went to London and joined the navy. In 1759 he became master of his own ship. In 1762 he married Elizabeth Betts, 13 years his junior. She spent only four months with her husband in their London home before he went back to sea. On his first expedition to the Pacific (1768–1771) he sailed around New Zealand in the Endeavour, which also came from Whitby, and 'discovered' the eastern coast of Australia. He landed at Botany Bay, south of Sydney. He circumnavigated the world and came back via the Cape of Good Hope. On his second expedition (1772–1775) he sailed south of the Antarctic Circle. On his third voyage, he 'discovered' Hawaii. He then tried to find a sea route from the Pacific north of Canada. There was too much ice and he had to stop. He returned to Hawaii to pick up food and water, but the islanders didn't understand him and killed him.

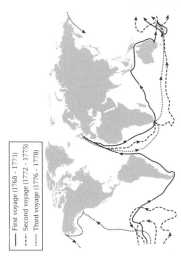

C Tour 36: The Captain Cook Country Tour

70 miles; whole day circular drive
Route directions

1 The drive starts at the Captain Cook Birthplace Museum in Marton. James was born here on October 27, 1728.

2 Take the A1772 and B1292 to Great Ayton and the Captain Cook Schoolroom Museum. Cook attended this school between 1736 and 1740. After that, he helped his father on the farm.

3 While in Great Ayton, visit All Saints Church. His mother and five of his seven brothers and sisters are buried in the churchyard.

4 Also admire the James Cook sculpture, which shows him at the age of 16 when he left Great Ayton for Staithes.

5 Take the four-mile 'Cook's Boyhood Walk' or drive to Gribdale, where you will find the Cook Monument, erected in 1827.

6 Take the A171 via Guisborough to the historic port of Whitby. Visit the Captain Cook Memorial Museum and a replica of Cook's ship Endeavour. Follow in Cook's path and join a trip around the harbour, or along the coast to the tiny fishing village of Staithes.

7 Alternatively, take the A174 coast road to Staithes. Visit the Captain Cook and Staithes Heritage Centre and look at 62 original paintings by Webber, the expedition artist on Cook's third voyage (1776–1779).

8 Pick up the A171 again at Guisborough for your return to Marton.

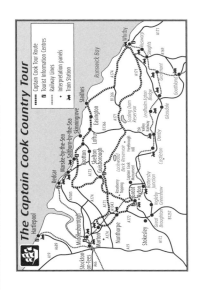

The Frog Prince – in the 21st century

LEVEL
Upper-intermediate

TOPIC
A modern version
of a traditional tale

ACTIVITY TYPE
Ordering a story

**READING
FOCUS**
Text organisation,
identifying
differences between
the modern and
traditional tale

TIME
40–50 minutes

KEY LANGUAGE
fairy tale,
politically correct,
real-estate,
developer, sexism,
sexual harassment,
spell, traditional

Past tenses

PREPARATION
One photocopy for
each pair of students –
cut into nine strips,
with the final strip kept
separate

Warm up

1 Ask students what they know about Grimms' fairy tale *The Frog Prince*. Use the Notes below to confirm or correct what students say.

2 Explain to students that they are going to read a modern version of the story. Encourage them to suggest how the story might be different from the traditional version.

Main activity

1 Give each pair of students the jumbled story. Tell students to put the sections of the story in order. When they have done this, they can compare their order with another pair.

2 Check the order with the class. Read aloud the first sentence or phrase of each section in order. Explain that *real-estate developers* sell property and are not really respected.

3 Ask students what are the main differences between the two versions of the tale. Elicit that the frog turns out to be a rather unattractive real-estate developer instead of a prince, and that the princess discovers this when he rescues her ball and not at her castle.

4 Explain to the class that the final part of the story is missing. Students, working in their pairs again, decide upon and write the final part of the story.

5 Get students to read out their ending to the class. Discuss the suggestions with the class. Give each student the final part of the story so that they can compare their version with the writer's.

6 Explain to the class that the modern version of the tale comes from a book called *Politically Correct Bedtime Stories*. Elicit or explain that if someone is *politically correct*, they believe that language and actions which could be offensive to others should be avoided. For example, the spelling of *womyn* in the story doesn't include the word *men*.

7 Ask students to read the story again and find examples of political (in)correctness.

> **Answer key**
> *sexism* – **paragraph 1**: the male power structure at her castle; the role of the eco-feminist warrior; **paragraph 2**: dreaming of the utopia that her queendom could become if womyn were in the position of power; **paragraph 6**: whether sexual harassment could take place between species
> *animal rights* – **paragraph 3**: I would never enslave a member of another species to work for my selfish desires; **paragraph 4**: your views on physical attraction between the species **paragraph 5**: my frog form is no better or worse – only different – than my human form
> *looks* – **paragraph 6**: vertically challenged
> *classism* – **paragraph 7**: don't sorcerers usually cast their spells on *princes*?

8 Ask students to find other examples of modern-day behaviour. For example: paragraph 2: *She didn't cry, of course, but she made a mental note to be more careful next time,* paragraph 3: *The frog said, 'Well, what if we make a deal on a contingency basis?'* paragraph 8: everything about the real-estate developer.

Follow up

● Ask students to suggest modern variations for other traditional tales.

> **Notes**
> A princess drops a golden ball into a spring. A frog offers to get it for her if she will love him. She assumes that he is talking nonsense, and agrees; he dives and fetches the ball. She goes off home with the ball, ignoring her promise to the frog. The next day, the frog arrives at the castle. The king makes the princess keep her promise. The frog is allowed to eat off her plate, and even to sleep in her bedroom. There, she tries to kill him. However, in the end, when the princess kisses the frog, he turns into a handsome prince. He explains that he was turned into a frog by a witch and only the princess could rescue him. Next day, they both set off for the prince's kingdom.

Once there was a young princess who, when she grew tired of beating her head against the male power structure at her castle, would relax by walking into the woods and sitting beside a small pond. There she would amuse herself by tossing her favourite golden ball up and down, and pondering the role of the eco-feminist warrior in her era.

One day, while she was dreaming of the utopia that her queendom could become if womyn were in the position of power, she dropped the ball, which rolled into the pond. The pond was so deep and murky she couldn't see where it had gone. She didn't cry, of course, but she made a mental note to be more careful next time.

Suddenly, she heard a voice say, 'I can get your ball for you, princess.'

She looked round, and saw the head of a frog popping above the surface of the pond. 'No, no,' she said, 'I would never enslave a member of another species to work for my selfish desires.'

The frog said, 'Well, what if we make a deal on a contingency basis? I'll get your ball for you if you do me a favour in return?'

The princess gladly agreed to this most equitable arrangement. The frog dived into the water and soon emerged with the golden ball in his mouth. He spat the ball on the bank and said, 'Now that I've done you a favour, I'd like to explore your views on physical attraction between the species.'

The princess couldn't imagine what the frog was talking about. The frog continued, 'You see, I am not really a frog at all. I'm really a man, but an evil sorcerer has cast a spell on me. While my frog form is no better or worse – only different – than my human form, I would so much like to be among people again. And the only thing that can break this spell is a kiss from a princess.'

The princess thought for a moment about whether sexual harassment could take place between species, but her heart went out to the frog for his predicament. She bent down and kissed the frog on the forehead. Instantly the frog grew and changed. And there, standing in the water where the frog had been, was a man in a golf shirt and loud plaid trousers – middle-aged, vertically challenged, and losing a little bit of hair on top.

The princess was taken aback. 'I'm sorry if this sounds a little classist,' she stammered, 'but ... what I mean to say is ... don't sorcerers usually cast their spells on *princes*?'

'Ordinarily, yes,' he said, 'but this time the target was just an innocent businessman. You see, I'm a real-estate developer, and the sorcerer thought I was cheating him in a property-line dispute. So he invited me out for a round of golf, and just as I was about to tee off, he transformed me. But my time as a frog wasn't wasted, you know. I've got to know every inch of these woods, and I think it would be ideal for an office/property share/resort complex. The location's great and the numbers add up perfectly! The bank wouldn't lend any money to a frog, but now that I'm in human form again, they'll be eating out of my hand. Oh, that will be sweet! And let me tell you, this is going to be a big project! Just drain the pond, cut down about 80 per cent of the trees, get easements for ...'

The frog developer was cut short when the princess shoved her golden ball back into his mouth. She then pushed him back underwater and held him there until he stopped thrashing. As she walked back to the castle, she marvelled at the number of good deeds that a person could do in just one morning. And while someone might have noticed that the frog was gone, no one ever missed the real estate developer.

17.1

Last man on the moon

LEVEL
Elementary

TOPIC
Space exploration

ACTIVITY TYPE
Reading
comprehension

**READING
FOCUS**
Scanning for specific
words, recognising
main ideas

TIME
40–50 minutes

KEY LANGUAGE
*astronaut, hatch,
helmet, lunar dust,
mission, moon buggy,
orbit, pilot, solar
system, spacecraft,
visor*

PREPARATION
One photocopy for
each student – with the
heading *Last man on
the moon 17.1* cut off
and then cut into two
parts (the text and the
Exercise)

Warm up

1 Revise and/or pre-teach the space words in Key language. Write the word *astronaut* on the
board. Elicit or explain the meaning of *astronaut*. Repeat this procedure with the other
words in the list. Explain that these words are all in the text students are going to read.
Encourage them to predict the topic of the text (space exploration).

Main activity

1 Give each student the text. Allow them one minute to find the names of six people in the
text. Then ask them which name features most often in the text.

> **Answer key**
> Neil Armstrong, Tom Hanks, Eugene Cernan, Edwin Aldrin, Harrison Schmitt,
> Tracy [Cernan]
> Eugene Cernan is the name which features most often.

2 Write the following heading on the board: *The _____ man on the moon*. Ask students to
read the text and complete the heading. While they are working, write *first, last, next* on
the board. Elicit that the text is about *The last man on the moon*.

3 Look at the photo with the class. Elicit that this shows Eugene Cernan at Cape Kennedy.
Ask students what he is holding in his hands. Elicit *helmet* and *visor*.

4 Ask students to read the text again and decide which paragraphs talk about the lunar trip
of a) the first man on the moon, b) the last man on the moon, and c) the next man on the
moon. Encourage students to work together in pairs so that they can help each other.

5 Check the answers with the class.

> **Answer key**
> **a)** paragraphs 1 and 4   **b)** paragraphs 2, 4, 5 and 6   **c)** paragraph 8

6 Write the following years on the board: *1963, 1966, 1969, 1972, 1995*. Ask students to say
what happened in these years.

7 Give each student the Exercise. Ask students to choose the correct sentence endings.

> **Answer key**
> **1** a **2** e **3** h **4** l

8 Students write sentences using information from the incorrect answers in the exercise.
Encourage stronger students to write a summary of Eugene Cernan's space career, using
all twelve sentences in a logical order.

> **Suggested answers**
> **c** Cernan trained first as a fighter pilot.
> **j** He started astronaut training in 1963.
> **a** Cernan's first space mission was in Gemini 9.
> **d** He crossed the coast of California.
> **k** While in orbit, he stepped into space to do some tests.
> **g** He walked in space for two hours and nine minutes.
> **b** Cernan's last mission was in Apollo 17 in 1972.
> **e** Apollo 17 landed in the Taurus–Littrow valley.
> **h** Cernan was on the moon for three days.
> **i** He took three trips, each seven hours long, in the moon buggy.
> **l** Before he took off from the moon, he wrote TC in the dust.
> **f** Future astronauts will head to Mars.

Follow up

● Ask students if they would like to go into space. How do they feel about space tourism?

● Encourage students to find further information about Eugene Cernan on his website:
www.genecernan.com. They can also find out more about space exploration on this
website: www.jsc.nasa.gov.

In his book *The Last Man on the Moon*, Cernan describes the walk: 'When the hatch stood open, I climbed out. Half my body stuck out of Gemini 9, and I rode along like a sightseeing bum on a boxcar. This was like sitting on God's front porch. We crossed the coast of California in the full flare of the morning sun, and in a single glance I could see from San Francisco to halfway across Mexico.'

By 1972, however, there was no longer much interest in space exploration. The space race between the US and the USSR was won when Armstrong and Edwin Aldrin landed on the moon in July 1969. Nasa knew that Apollo 17 would be the last mission, for both the Apollo programme and for Cernan. The Apollo 17 mission landed on the moon on December 11 three years later.

The world will always remember the words of the first man on the moon. On July 21, 1969, Neil Armstrong stepped onto the moon's surface and announced: 'That's one small step for [a] man, one giant leap for mankind.' People also know about Apollo 13 – they have seen the 1995 film in which Tom Hanks and two fellow actor-astronauts were saved from disaster. But, can anyone name the last man on the moon? Probably not.

The little-known Eugene Cernan was the last man on the moon. His trip in 1972 came at the end of a great career in space. He trained first as a fighter pilot before he started astronaut training in 1963. Three years later, he piloted Gemini 9. While in orbit, he stepped into space to do some tests. But there were problems, and Cernan began breathing heavily and perspiring. Water vapour built up inside his helmet and froze over his visor. Cernan couldn't see, but he remained calm. He walked in space for two hours and nine minutes, at that time the longest space walk anyone had ever done.

Cernan and his fellow astronaut Harrison Schmitt landed in a steep lunar valley named Taurus-Littrow. They then spent three days on the moon and took three trips, each seven hours long, on the moon buggy.

Before leaving, Cernan left what he hoped would be a lasting mark: 'With a single finger, I scratched my daughter Tracy's initials in the lunar dust, knowing that they would remain there undisturbed for more years than anyone could imagine.'

That, however, may be less time than Cernan expected. A spokesman for the European Space Agency said: "The moon is again a target. We see it as a springboard to future exploration of the solar system."

When future astronauts take off from the moon, they will probably head not back to Earth but to Mars.

Exercise

Choose the correct ending for each sentence.

1 Cernan's first space mission was
  a in Gemini 9.
  b in Apollo 17 in 1972.
  c as a fighter pilot.

2 Apollo 17
  d crossed the coast of California.
  e landed in the Taurus–Littrow valley.
  f will head to Mars.

3 Cernan was on the moon for
  g two hours and nine minutes.
  h three days.
  i seven hours.

4 Before he took off from the moon, he
  j started astronaut training.
  k stepped into space to do some tests.
  l wrote TC in the dust.

17.2

Flame and fortune

LEVEL
Intermediate

TOPIC
Re-use of steelworks
as science adventure
park

ACTIVITY TYPE
Reading
comprehension

**READING
FOCUS**
Skimming for gist,
reading for specific
information

TIME
40–50 minutes

KEY LANGUAGE
*apprentice, armaments,
attraction, battleships,
exhibits, furnaces,
gadgets, gyroscopic chair,
hi-tech, molten metal,
tanks, wind tunnel*

PREPARATION
One photocopy for each
student

Warm up

1 Ask students which countries in the world are the main steel producers. Is steel produced in their country? Where is the nearest steelworks?

> **Answer key**
> US, Russia, Ukraine and Japan are the main steel producers.

2 Write the twelve words from Key language on the board in random order. Ask students to decide which six words are associated with *steelworks*. Encourage them to work in pairs so that they can help each other and to use their dictionaries if necessary.

3 Check the answers with the class. Then ask students what the other six words might be associated with.

> **Answer key**
> | **steelworks** | apprentice   armaments   battleships   furnaces molten metal   tanks |
> | **science adventure park** | attraction   exhibits   gadgets   gyroscopic chair hi-tech   wind tunnel |

4 Read out the title and bi-line of the article *Flame and fortune: Stephen McClarence is fired up by a Sheffield steelworks reborn as a hi-tech science adventure playground*. Ask students to paraphrase the title and bi-line. Elicit that the article is about the past and the present.

Main activity

1 Give each student a photocopy. Allow students two minutes to read the text and decide if each paragraph refers to the steelworks or to the science adventure park. Point out that two paragraphs refer to both the steelworks and the science adventure park, and one paragraph refers to neither of them.

2 On the board, write the three column headings from Answer key to help students begin to build up their own chart. Ask students to read the text again and find figures and dates. They decide if these refer to the steelworks or to the science adventure park.

3 Students read the text again and find the names of people. Again, they decide if these refer to the steelworks or to the science adventure park, or to both.

> **Answer key**
> **1** steelworks – paragraph 2   science adventure park – paragraphs 4, 5, 7
>   both – paragraphs 1, 3   neither – paragraph 6
>
> | **2 steelworks** | **science adventure park** | **both** |
> |---|---|---|
> | employed 10,000 people | cost £46m | third of a mile long |
> | Chris Silvester started | aims to attract 300,000 visitors | nine storeys high |
> | work in 1967 | a year | |
> | closed in 1993 | | |
> | **3** James Callaghan | Stephen Feber, Tim Caulton | Chris Silvester |

4 Students decide which paragraphs refer to the past and which to the present. Point out that some paragraphs refer to both.

> **Answer key**
> **past** – paragraph 2   **present** – paragraphs 1, 4, 5, 7   **both** – 3, 6

5 Discuss with the class the contrasts between past and present made in the article. Everyone will probably agree that these are between: 1) the past and present use of the steelworks, 2) Chris Silvester's past and present jobs, 3) children, past and present.

Follow up

- Ask students if they know any places that have been re-used in a different way.

- Ask students if they would be interested in going to Magna. What could they do and see there? Encourage students to find further information about the museum on its website: www.magna-trust.org.uk.

Flame and fortune

Stephen McClarence is fired up by a Sheffield steelworks reborn as a hi-tech science adventure playground

Magna, as staff at the UK's 'first science adventure park' sometimes have to tell puzzled callers, is Latin for 'big'. And big it is. The £46 million centre fills a once-derelict South Yorkshire steelworks a third of a mile long and nine storeys high.

For most of the last century, its furnaces made steel for battleships, tanks and other armaments. In its heyday, it employed 10,000 people, and the then Prime Minister James Callaghan sent a Christmas card in the Seventies, thanking everyone who had made it the world's most productive steelworks (they still have the card). The flames, sparks and flashes from its white-hot molten metal lit up the night sky between Sheffield and Rotherham.

Chris Silvester started work there as an apprentice in 1967. He was made redundant when the works closed in 1993. Now he is back, as a technician at Magna. Silvester describes the unnerving experience of stepping back into a workplace he thought he would never see again: 'I went up to my old office, and there was my locker. My overalls and donkey jacket still hung inside, just as I'd left them in 1993. It was a bit spooky really. Once you're out of a place like a steelworks, you miss having a proper job. I worked in retail for a bit, but this was a man's world.'

Magna aims to attract 300,000 visitors a year, promises 'exhibits that cough, snore, fart and belch', and puts great emphasis on 'the wow factor' and fun. Part of that fun, a 'fire tornado', is charging itself up. Suddenly it flares. A column of flames shoots 20ft into the air, and fans suck it into a fierce, roaring spiral. Standing 10ft away behind a barrier, you can feel the keen heat on your face. The tornado is the sort of spectacle Magna hopes will pull in the crowds.

The museum takes the four elements of earth, air, fire and water as the starting point for 'an adventure playground of science that shows how the world works'. 'We're not a museum of the steel industry,' says chief executive Stephen Feber. 'We're about the present and the future. We're going to be a new kind of attraction. We want to make science and technology accessible.'

Pinned to his office wall is a photograph of the cluttered garage workshop where his father showed him the wonders of science as a child in Woodford Green, east London. 'The environment kids inhabit today is less rich than mine was,' he says. 'They don't play out, they don't travel alone, they don't make things for themselves. Their world has contracted, while the TV and digital world has expanded.'

Children are central to Magna. 'It's a family day out,' says development director Tim Caulton. They will love the interactive hands-on gadgets at Magna – wind tunnels that show how it feels to fly, artificial cornfields that show how nature reacts to strong winds. 'You can have fun and education at the same time,' continues Caulton, as he pumps a machine that sends geysers of boiling water spurting to the roof, and clambers on a gyroscopic chair that spins him round like a human top.

17.3

Idiotic inventions … and products we could live without

LEVEL
Upper-intermediate

TOPIC
Daft inventions

ACTIVITY TYPE
Reading a text and choosing a title, using the title to work out the content of another text

READING FOCUS
Extracting key information, asking and answering questions about a text, recreating a text

TIME
40–50 minutes

KEY LANGUAGE
Past tenses

PREPARATION
One photocopy for each pair of students – cut down the middle

Warm up

1 Explain to students that they are going to read about and discuss inventions. Ask students to name some of the most important and useful inventions ever and to say what they know about them.

2 Explain that students are actually going to read about idiotic inventions, things produced by people who didn't ask *Is it useful? Will anyone need it? Do people really want a combined lemon squeezer and fly trap?*

3 Ask students if they know of any idiotic inventions. For example, have they heard of the artificial spray-on dirt which a German firm invented for city-dwellers who only use their four-wheel-drive vehicles on congested city roads?

Main activity

1 Divide the class into two. Give each student in one half the Student A column of the photocopy and each student in the other half the Student B column. Explain that the four titles at the top of the boxes belong to the numbered texts on the other half of the photocopy.

2 Students read each of their four descriptions and choose a title for each invention. Encourage students to work together in pairs so that they can help each other. Tell them that they can only use words from the description itself in their title. Do not check the answers at this point.

3 Students continue working in pairs. They use the headings at the top of their half of the photocopy to predict what the other four inventions are. They also think about the questions they need to ask to find out more about the inventions.

4 Divide the class into different pairs so that each person is working with someone who has read the other four descriptions. Students take turns to tell their partner what they think the other four inventions are. They also ask questions to find out further details. Point out that they must not mention the exact title when they say what they know or ask questions. For example, a student can use the word *bumper* and *pedestrian*, but not *pedestrian bumper*. Similarly, *medicine-spoon* and *chocolate* are possible, but not *chocolate medicine-spoon*.

5 Ask students to name the titles they have chosen. Their partner can confirm whether or not these are the same as those at the top of the column.

6 Give each student the descriptions they haven't read. Ask them to underline any new information they didn't find out from their partner.

Follow up

• Discuss the inventions with the class. Which do students think is the most idiotic invention? Which might they have found useful?

• Encourage students to find further information about idiotic inventions on this website: www.funnyscheidt.freeservers.com/dumb.html.

Student A

Pedestrian bumper
Musical bra
Dog glasses
Floating soap

1 ....

In 1937 the aptly named Constance Honey of Chelsea, London patented a chocolate spoon for giving medicine to reluctant children. Basically, her idea failed because it was too popular. She would tell her young relatives: 'I'd give you your medicine, but I haven't a spoon left in the house.'

3 ....

'It is well known that cooling the top of the head will have a cooling effect on the entire person,' stated Chicago's Harold W. Dahly in his 1967 patent for solar-cooled headgear. Unfortunately, any benefits of the hat, which operated by means of a solar-powered fan inside the top, were outweighed by the fact that it made the wearer look totally ridiculous.

5 ....

This hygienic item was designed in 1959 by Milwaukee inventor Bertha Dlugi in response to what she obviously thought was a problem: Pet birds were often allowed to fly through an owner's house, yet 'These birds cannot normally be house-trained as other pets are, and their excremental discharge is frequently deposited on household furnishings when they are at liberty, creating an unsanitary condition.' The answer to this? The bird diaper, a triangular patch of material attached to a harness that you can put around your pet parakeet.

7 ....

In 1919 John Humphrey of Connecticut invented an unusual alarm clock, one which would rouse a sleeper from his slumbers by hitting him. The apparatus consisted of a timepiece attached to an adjustable rod with a rubber ball on the end. When the alarm on the clock went off, instead of a bell ringing, the rod would be activated, causing the ball to hit the desired area of the sleeper's anatomy. Humphrey deemed his device to be of great benefit to people who might be upset by bells ... but presumably not by being whacked over the head with a ball.

Student B

Chocolate medicine-spoon
Solar-cooled hat
Bird diaper
Hitting clock

2 ....

To reduce pedestrian casualties in 1960, David Gutman from Philadelphia came up with a special bumper designed to be fixed to the front of a car. Not only would it cushion the impact, but it also had a huge pair of claws which would grab the pedestrian around the waist to prevent him dropping to the street.

4 ....

This bra was created to honour Mozart on the two hundredth anniversary of his death and was manufactured by Japanese lingerie maker Triumph International. The bra contains a memory chip that plays a twenty second selection of Mozart's musical works and also has lights that flash in time as the music plays. One drawback: the bra isn't washable, so it's not for everyday wear.

6 ....

Do you ever worry about Fido's eyesight? This invention, patented by a French optician in 1975, is the answer. The inventor developed them after she made sunglasses for her own dog. Just like glasses for people, they can be adjusted to different visual deficiencies – there are corrective lenses for myopic dogs; glasses for dogs recuperating from cataracts; even protective ones against wind and dust for dogs who hang their heads out of car windows.

8 ....

British housewife Sarah Fox found bathtimes a nightmare with four small children. The bars of soap turned gooey as they slipped underwater and then the youngsters slipped on them when standing to get out. So Sarah set out to make a floating soap. Early attempts – including inserting a table-tennis ball inside a soap bar – sank without trace, but then she hit on a buoyancy technique. This involved grating soap, microwaving it and finally putting it through a food processor. Sarah and her husband ploughed cash into marketing attempts, but shops showed no interest and the big soap companies did not even reply to her letters. In 1992 she was forced to abandon the project.

18.1

How much do you know about ... earthquakes?

LEVEL
Elementary

TOPIC
Earthquakes

ACTIVITY TYPE
Problem-solving
through pairwork
question-and-answer

**READING
FOCUS**
Identifying missing
information

TIME
40–50 minutes

KEY LANGUAGE
Numbers, dates, places
Present simple, past
simple

PREPARATION
One photocopy for
each pair of students –
cut into two parts
(student A text and
student B text)

Warm up

1 Explain to students that they are going to read about and discuss earthquakes. Ask students what they already know about earthquakes. Where have there been earthquakes?

2 Practise numbers and dates with the class. Write four figures on the board with a comma after the first number, e.g. *1,702*. Invite students to say the number (*one thousand, seven hundred and two*). Then rub out the comma and invite students to say the date (*seventeen oh two*). Practise some long numbers, e.g. 110,000 (*one hundred and ten thousand*).

Main activity

1 Divide the class into two. Give each student in one half the Student A text and each student in the other half the Student B text. Tell students to read the first paragraph and try to work out what kind of information is missing. Elicit that a number is missing from (1) and a place from (2). Ask students to suggest the questions they need to ask in order to find out the missing information.

2 Tell students to read their text and write the questions they need to ask. Encourage students to work together in pairs or small groups so that they can help each other.

3 Divide the class into different pairs so that each student is working with someone who has read the other text. Partners take turns to ask and answer questions.

4 Check the answers with the class. Individual students ask and answer questions.

Answer key	
1 What per cent (of earthquakes) occur in the ring of fire?	ninety
2 Where does the Alpine Belt start?	Spain
3 Where was the worst earthquake so far recorded?	off the coast of Colombia
4 When was the worst earthquake so far recorded?	1906
5 How many earthquakes are there every year?	about a million
6 How often does a large earthquake occur?	about every two weeks
7 When was the earthquake?	1985
8 How far (away) from Mexico is Houston?	1,609 kilometres away
9 How many people did the earthquake kill?	830,000
10 When was the earthquake?	1976
11 How long did the earthquake last?	seven minutes
12 How wide were the cracks in the ground?	90 centimetres
13 When was the earthquake?	1979
14 How far did the avalanche fall?	4,000 metres
15 Which town did it bury?	Yungay
16 How many people did the avalanche kill?	18,000
17 Where was the earthquake in 1906?	San Francisco, USA
18 How long did the fire last?	three and a half days
19 How long does an earthquake usually last?	less than one minute
20 Where was the earthquake in 1755?	Lisbon, Portugal

5 Students continue working with their partner. They have to list the dates and places of the earthquakes in order, starting with the earliest.

Answer key		
1556 Shanxi province, China	1906 San Francisco	1979 Peru
1755 Lisbon, Portugal	1964 Alaska	1985 Mexico
1906 Colombia	1976 Tangshan province, China	

Follow up

● Students play a memory game in teams. They take turns to ask questions about the earthquakes in the list.

● Encourage students to find further information about earthquakes on this website: www.earthquake.usgs.gov/4kids/.

Student A

Earthquakes happen on land and under the sea. (1) ...... per cent occur in the 'ring of fire', which circles the Pacific Ocean. Many others occur along the Alpine Belt, which starts in Spain in the west, and goes through the Himalayas as far as South-East Asia.

The magnitude or power of an earthquake is measured on the Richter Scale. Starting at 1, each number on the Scale is ten times more powerful than the number below. The worst earthquake so far recorded was 8.9 off the coast of (3) ...... in 1906.

There are about (5) ...... earthquakes every year – any vibration in the Earth's crust is an earthquake. A large earthquake occurs about every two weeks – mostly under the sea, where it does little harm.

The shock of an earthquake can sometimes be felt hundreds of kilometres away. Water splashed in swimming pools in Houston, USA after the earthquake in Mexico in (7) ...... – 1,609 km away.

China has the worst record for earthquake deaths. In 1556, an earthquake killed (9) ...... people in Shanxi province. In 1976, the earthquake in Tangshan province – 8.2 on the Richter Scale – killed 750,000 people.

The ground can roll like waves on the ocean in a very bad earthquake. The 1964 earthquake in Alaska lasted for (11) .... The shaking opened up huge cracks in the ground, up to 90 cm wide and 12 m deep. Many buildings tilted and slid down into the cracks.

The earthquake off the coast of Peru in (13) ...... caused an avalanche of snow and rock on land – high on the Nevados Huascaran mountain. The avalanche fell 4,000 m. It buried the town of (15) ...... under 10 m of rock and killed at least 18,000 people.

Huge fires can break out after an earthquake. In 1906, after the earthquake in (17) ...... , fire destroyed the wooden buildings of the city. The water pipes burst during the earthquake, so the fire lasted for three and a half days. But nine years later, the city had been rebuilt.

An earthquake usually lasts for less than (19) .... The earthquake in Lisbon, Portugal, in 1755 lasted for ten minutes, and the shock waves were felt as far away as North Africa.

Student B

Earthquakes happen on land and under the sea. Ninety per cent occur in the 'ring of fire', which circles the Pacific Ocean. Many others occur along the Alpine Belt, which starts in (2) ...... in the west, and goes through the Himalayas as far as South-East Asia.

The magnitude or power of an earthquake is measured on the Richter Scale. Starting at 1, each number on the Scale is ten times more powerful than the number below. The worst earthquake so far recorded was 8.9 off the coast of Columbia in (4) ....

There are about a million earthquakes every year – any vibration in the Earth's crust is an earthquake. A large earthquake occurs about every (6) ...... – mostly under the sea, where it does little harm.

The shock of an earthquake can sometimes be felt hundreds of kilometres away. Water splashed in swimming pools in Houston, USA after the earthquake in Mexico in 1985 – (8) ...... km away.

China has the worst record for earthquake deaths. In 1556, an earthquake killed 830,000 people in Shanxi province. In (10) ...... , the earthquake in Tangshan province – 8.2 on the Richter Scale – killed 750,000 people.

The ground can roll like waves on the ocean in a very bad earthquake. The 1964 earthquake in Alaska lasted for seven minutes. The shaking opened up huge cracks in the ground, up to (12) ...... cm wide and 12 m deep. Many buildings tilted and slid down into the cracks.

The earthquake off the coast of Peru in 1979 caused an avalanche of snow and rock on land – high on the Nevados Huascaran mountain. The avalanche fell (14) ...... m. It buried the town of Yungay under 10 m of rock and killed at least (16) ...... people.

Huge fires can break out after an earthquake. In 1906, after the earthquake in San Francisco, USA, fire destroyed the wooden buildings of the city. The water pipes burst during the earthquake, so the fire lasted for (18) .... But nine years later, the city had been rebuilt.

An earthquake usually lasts for less than one minute. The earthquake in (20) ...... , in 1755 lasted for ten minutes, and the shock waves were felt as far away as North Africa.

18.2

Mummy, oh Mummy

LEVEL
Intermediate

TOPIC
Pollution

ACTIVITY TYPE
Ordering lines in a poem

READING FOCUS
Text organisation, understanding the main message

TIME
30–40 minutes

KEY LANGUAGE
foam fumes, mattress, plastic, pop bottles and tins, spraying crops, sweet papers, tar

PREPARATION
One photocopy for each pair or group of three students – cut into two parts (the pictures and the poem cut into sixteen pairs of lines)

Warm up

1 Explain to students that they are going to read about and discuss pollution.

2 Write these three questions on the board:
1 What's pollution?
2 Who or what causes pollution?
3 What will happen if pollution goes on?

3 Divide the class into groups of three. Students discuss the questions. Give each group a set of the pictures to stimulate discussion.

4 Discuss the questions with the class. Use the pictures to teach *fumes* and *foam* (a), *tar* (b), *spraying crops* (c), *mattress* (d), *plastics, pop bottles* and *tins* (e), *sweet papers* (f).

Main activity

1 Give each group of students a set of jumbled pairs of lines.

2 Read out the first verse of the poem, beginning with *Mummy, oh Mummy, what's this pollution* and ending with *Before we get back in the car*. Students order the four pairs of lines. Make sure that everyone has the lines in the correct order (as in the top left-hand part of the photocopy).

3 Use the questions below to discuss the verse.

Questions	Answer key
1 How many people are speaking?	**1** two
2 Who are they?	**2** a child and his/her mother
3 How many lines does the child speak?	**3** two
4 What marks the beginning and ending of the speakers' words?	**4** speech marks
5 How is what the mother says in her first four lines different from what she says in her last two?	**5** the last two go against what she has just said
6 What do you notice about the last words in the second and fourth lines? And in the sixth and eighth lines?	**6** they rhyme

4 Explain that the poem has three more verses. Students order the lines of the other three verses and then decide on the order of the three verses.

5 Read the other three verses out loud, beginning with *Mummy, oh Mummy, who makes pollution*, and ending with *We're just enjoying our day*. Students check that they have correctly ordered the lines.

6 Encourage students to work out that *'cos* is a short form of *because* and that *belching* is used here to mean *producing*. If you like, explain that *belch* means *allow air from the stomach to come out noisily through the mouth*.

7 Students discuss the message of the poem in their pairs or groups. They then write a one-sentence summary of the poem's message.

8 Students read their sentences to the class. Everyone will probably agree that the poem not only talks about pollution and its harmful effects on the environment, but its main message is that we think that preventing pollution is the responsibility of others.

Follow up

● Students work in pairs or groups and write a conversation between the child and his/her mother about another thing which is not good for us or for the environment, e.g. smoking, eating chocolate, using cars rather than buses, bikes or walking. Encourage them to use the structure of the verses: the child's question, the mother's sensible answer, her contradiction. They can then read out their conversation to the rest of the class.

'Mummy, oh Mummy, what's this pollution
That everyone's talking about?'

'Mummy, oh Mummy, what's going to happen
If all the pollution goes on?'

'Pollution's the mess that the country is in,
That we'd all be far better without.

'Well all the world will end up like a second-hand
    junk-yard,
With all of its treasures quite gone.

It's factories belching their fumes in the air,
And the beaches all covered with tar,

The fields will be littered with plastics and tins,
The streams will be covered with foam,

Now throw all those sweet papers into the bushes
Before we get back in the car.'

Now throw those two pop bottles over the hedge,
Save us from carrying them home.'

'Mummy, oh Mummy, who makes pollution,
And why don't they stop if it's bad?'

'But Mummy, oh Mummy, if I throw the bottles,
Won't that be polluting the wood?'

''Cos people like that just don't think about others,
They don't think at all, I might add.

'Nonsense! that isn't the same thing at all,
You just shut up and be good.

They spray all the crops and they poison the flowers,
And wipe out the birds and the bees,

If you're going to start getting silly ideas
I'm taking you home right away,

Now there's a good place we could dump that old
    mattress
Right out of sight in the trees.'

'Cos pollution is something that other folk do,
We're just enjoying our day.'

18.3

LEVEL
Upper-intermediate

TOPIC
Lawyer jokes

ACTIVITY TYPE
Matching punch lines
with joke situations

READING FOCUS
Text cohesion,
paraphrasing

TIME
40–50 minutes

KEY LANGUAGE
*acquitted, burglary,
charged, counsel for
the prosecution,
damages, evidence,
forgery, guilty,
innocent, judge,
judgement, jury,
lawyer, litigation,
murder, negligence,
punch line, sentenced,
theft, witness*

PREPARATION
One photocopy for
each group of three
students – cut into two
parts (the Situations and
the Punch lines, with the
Punch lines cut into ten
strips)

Guilty!

Warm up

1 Revise and/or pre-teach words associated with crime and law. Ask students to name crimes, e.g. *burglary*, *murder*. Explain *forgery* and *theft*. Then ask what happens if someone is *charged* with such a crime; they are put on trial in a court. Ask which people are present in a court, e.g. *judge*, *jury*. Explain *lawyer, counsel for the prosecution, witness*. Ask what happens after the jury has heard the *evidence*. Elicit that the person is found *guilty* and *sentenced*, or *innocent* and *acquitted*. Remind students that other types of cases are discussed in court, e.g. suing someone for *negligence*, or *litigation* between two neighbours. Explain that *judgement* will be given to one party, and that *damages* will be awarded.

2 Explain to students that they are going to read and discuss some jokes about crime and law. They have to match the punch lines with the situations. Give one or two examples of jokes with punch lines.

> **Jokes**
> 1 *'Is there a criminal lawyer in town?'*   *'I think so, but I can't prove it.'*
> 2 *'Does your lawyer know the law?'*   *'I don't know, but he knows the judge.'*

Main activity

1 Give each group of three students the Situations.

2 Discuss the first joke with the class. Explain that the *punch line* is something that the lawyer said. Some of his words come before *said the lawyer* and some come after. Read out the punch line replacing … with *said the lawyer*.

3 Students work in their groups and predict the punch lines. They write their punch lines in a list.

4 Give each group of students a set of Punch lines. Tell students to match the punch lines with the situations. The punch lines should be ordered as shown on the worksheet.

5 Check the answers with the class. Get a group of three students to read out each joke with its punch line. One student narrates the joke, another student reads out one person's words and the third student reads out the other person's words. For example:

> Student 1:   A client asked the lawyer who was defending him,
> Student 2:   'How long do you think this business is going to last?'
> Student 3:   'Well,'
> Student 1:   said the lawyer,
> Student 3:   'for me about three hours. For you, about three years.'

6 Ask students to paraphrase the punch lines.

> **Suggested answers**
> 1 For me about three hours in court. For you, about three years in prison.
> 2 The client is hoping to convince his lawyer that he wouldn't be able to write anyone's name.
> 3 The lawyer is saying that there is no point in having an accident unless you have a good lawyer who can win your case.
> 4 Mrs Robinson didn't want a fair settlement. She wanted her lawyer to get her more money than that.
> 5 The lawyer thinks that the client will get more damages if he goes to court on crutches.
> 6 We can all produce millions of witnesses to say that they didn't see us do something!
> 7 When the lawyer said 'leave it all to me', he means he will deal with the situation. Mrs Smith is referring to what will happen to her money after her death.
> 8 The husband doesn't think lawyers are honest – so for him 'a lawyer and an honest man' can't be one person.
> 9 The farmer ignored his lawyer's advice, but completely ruined his neighbour's chances of winning the litigation case.
> 10 With his question, the man has revealed his guilt to his lawyer.

Follow up

● Discuss the jokes with the class. Which do students particularly like?

Situations

1 A client asked the lawyer who was defending him, 'How long do you think this business is going to last?'
   '... ,' said the lawyer, '... .'

2 A man charged with forgery spoke to his lawyer. 'I can't even write my own name,' he protested.
   '... ,' said the counsel for the prosecution, '... .'

3 A lawyer won a case on behalf of a client who had sued his employers for negligence after falling down a lift shaft. When the client was presented with the bill, he was furious. 'You've taken most of my damages!' he stormed. 'How do you justify that?'
   'Because,' said the lawyer. 'I provided the skill, the knowledge and the legal expertise to win the case.'
   'But I provided the case itself,' protested the client.
   '... ,' said the lawyer arrogantly. '... .'

4 In a divorce case, a lawyer acting for the wife spoke to his client.
   'Well, Mrs Robinson,' he said, 'I have finally arrived at a settlement with your husband which I feel is fair to both of you.'
   '... ,' said the wife indignantly. '... .'

5 A man who had been hurt in a motor accident spent several weeks in hospital. After his release, he was hobbling along the street on crutches when he met an old friend. 'Hello, Jim,' said the friend. 'Glad to see you up and about again. How long will it be before you can get rid of those crutches?'
   '... ,' said Jim, '... .'

6 A farm labourer accused of the theft of a wheelbarrow protested his innocence in court. In examination, prosecuting counsel said, 'You say you are innocent, yet you have heard the evidence of two witnesses who swear that they saw you take the wheelbarrow.'
   '... ,' said the accused. '... .'

7 A woman visited her family lawyer and said, 'I'd like to go over my will again, Mr Jenks. I'm a bit worried about ...'
   'Don't worry, Mrs Smith,' said the lawyer, 'just leave it all to me.'
   '... ,' said Mrs Smith with a sigh. '... .'

8 A couple were walking through a cemetery. They stopped before a tombstone which bore the following inscription: 'Here lies a lawyer and an honest man.' The husband turned to his wife.
   '... ,' said the man, '... .'

9 A farmer was engaged in litigation against his neighbour. 'How would it be if I sent the judge a couple of nice, fat ducks?' the farmer asked his lawyer.
   'Don't you dare!' said the lawyer, aghast. 'That would completely ruin your chances.'
   The case came to court and judgement was given in favour of the farmer. The lawyer was surprised and said as much to his client.
   'Well, I expect it was the ducks that did it,' said the farmer with a grin. You don't mean to say you sent them after all!' exclaimed the lawyer.
   '... ,' said the farmer. '... .'

10 A man accused of stealing a watch was acquitted on insufficient evidence. He later asked his lawyer, 'What does "acquitted" mean?'
   'It means,' said his lawyer, 'that the court has found you innocent. You are free to go.'
   '... ,' said his client. '... .'

Punch lines

'Well,' ... , for me about three hours. For you, about three years.'

'Ah,' ... , 'but you're not charged with writing your own name.'

'Oh, that,' ... . 'Anybody can fall down a lift shaft.'

'Fair to both of us!' ... . 'I could have done that myself! Why do you think I hired a lawyer?'

'Well,' ... , 'my doctor says I can get along without them now, but my lawyer says I can't.'

'That's nothing,' ... . 'I can produce twelve witnesses who will swear that they didn't see me take it.'

'I suppose I may as well,' ... . 'You'll get it all in the end.'

'You wouldn't think there'd be room,' ... , 'for two men in such a small grave.'

'Yes, I did,' ... . 'But I sent them in the other chap's name.'

'I understand,' ... . 'That must mean that I can keep the watch.'

Also available in the Cambridge Copy Collection

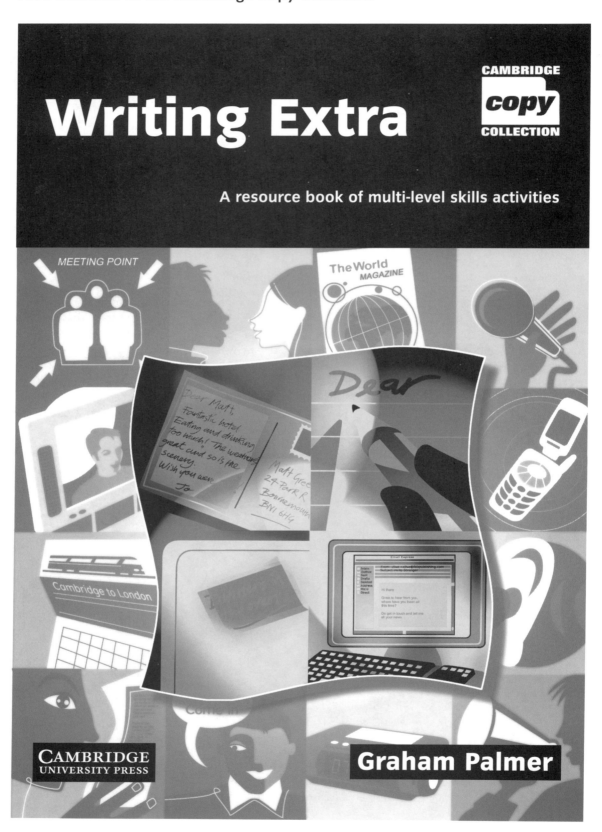

Writing Extra

CAMBRIDGE copy COLLECTION

A resource book of multi-level skills activities

CAMBRIDGE UNIVERSITY PRESS

Graham Palmer

ISBN 0 521 52387 6 Resource Book

Also available in the Cambridge Copy Collection

ISBN 0 521 75463 1 Resource Book

ISBN 0 521 75465 8 Audio CD

ISBN 0 521 75464 X Book and Audio CD Pack

Also available in the Cambridge Copy Collection

ISBN 0 521 75460 7 Resource Book

ISBN 0 521 75462 3 Audio CD

ISBN 0 521 75461 5 Book and Audio CD Pack